SINGING FOR MUSICALS

MUSICALS

A Practical Guide

Singing for Musicals

A Practical Guide

Millie Taylor

THE CROWOOD PRESS

First published in 2008 by
The Crowood Press Ltd
Ramsbury, Marlborough
Wiltshire SN8 2HR

www.crowood.com

British Library Cataloguing-in-Publication Data
A catalogue record for this book is available from the British Library.

ISBN 978 1 86126 993 5

Illustrations by Caroline Pratt

Typeset by Carolyn Griffiths

Printed and bound in Spain by GraphyCems

CONTENTS

INTRODUCTION

Do you sing in the bathroom? Do you enjoy releasing sound into the air and hearing it come back to you? What does it tell you about how you are feeling? It is a very different sensation to vocalize the song that is running around in your head, rather than just listening to it endlessly repeating in the silence of your brain. Take a breath, now, and blow out the air on an 'Aah'. Isn't that great? Don't you feel released, and bold, and bigger? Don't worry about who can hear you or even what it sounds like, just feel your body using breath and filling the room (the bathroom is usually good) with vibrations. Why is that so difficult? Why is it difficult to vocalize when not given permission to sing, either by singing along to a recording, or with others, or to piano or guitar accompaniment? Why are we so constrained?

As babies our vocal language begins when we explore the gurgles and raspberries, the giggles and burbles that come from our mouths and allow us to join in the sound and the conversation around us. As small children we make up songs, both wordless and then verbalized that accompany our playful activities and express our presence. Then we begin to be taught to sing the 'right' words and tune, to make the 'right' sounds, and our inhibitions are born. Soon we're being told to shush, though we're praised and applauded for doing a turn at the 'right' time. How many voices are silenced by the age of five? Where did the playfulness of gurgling and the joy of vocalizing our accompaniment to the world go?

One of the purposes of this book is to give you back the joy of using your voice in all its variety. In *Singing for Musicals*, you will be encouraged to sing 'in tune' and with the music, but you will also be encouraged to explore all the sounds of your voice and to enjoy the full range of sounds you can make. I can't begin to count the number of times professional performers, students in training, and amateur performers have told me 'I can't sing, I can get by with a character song, but I can't sing'. Well, of course you can sing. There are a very small number of people who have genuine physical or medical problems that affect the vocal mechanism and which might stop them singing. What you mean is that you are constrained from singing, worried about the sound you make and what people will think. The truth is that you practise speaking every day, so you are used to creating sound, hearing your voice, and articulating words in that way. Singing is simply a more extended form of that delivery, which requires more space and energy and can be more sustained. It, too, requires practice, partly so that you get used to using the muscles more strongly, but also so that you get used to hearing, feeling and shaping your sound, so that you start to enjoy exploring the sound of your voice, and so that you are comfortable letting others hear your voice and share the song.

It is often said that the eyes are the mirrors of the soul. I would add that the voice is the reflection of the body. You can read an awful lot about another person's physical and emotional state from the sound of their voice. It may be that you don't want to reveal yourself to others, but it is that capacity of the voice to reveal emotions and passions, and the mimetic ability of others to empathetically mirror those emotions, that makes the voice such a powerful instrument. The voice can touch others more than any other musical instrument through the vibrations of sound and the revelation of the singing body's tensions and resonances. Although we have the power to change the quality of our sound and sing in a variety of characters and styles, this doesn't alter the fact that the body and the emotions can be revealed and shared. This is, I believe, one of the principal reasons for the overwhelming importance of popular song and musical theatre in our everyday lives. We can touch others and we can be touched by the revelation of emotional stories in song.

SINGING IN A RANGE OF STYLES

If you listen to a range of music you will begin to recognize that the sound of the voice changes in accordance with the expectations of particular genres of music. These expectations of the sound of the voice are determined by culture, by the requirements of the music to be sung but, more than anything, by the authenticity required by the genre. Authenticity can mean many different things in different genres, but the term is most often used in relation to rock music, where the roughness of the sound, the ability to play instruments live, and the impression of 'true' emotion and working-class presentation are all prized. On the other hand, operatic voices need to be highly trained to respond to the demands of the music. This has led to particular aesthetic qualities that are then perceived as 'authentic' and 'natural' within that tradition. The result of this is that if you want to sing in musicals you need to sound like other musical-theatre singers, and this can encompass a wide range of sounds and materials but, in essence, there needs to be a relationship between the sound of your spoken and sung voices to the extent that your sung voice is an extension of your spoken voice, with the same accent and delivery, only altered by the pace and pitch of the music.

There are a number of factors that affect the relationship between words, music, vocal sound and vocal delivery that can help define different types of singing or musical style. In a chicken-and-egg fashion it is not clear whether the vocal style leads the music or the music inspires the vocal style, but in order to conform to a particular genre you need to be aware of the expectations of each type of singing. The other factor to consider is that musical theatre contains a range of musical styles, so you need to be able to adapt your vocal sound to the musical expectations. Listen to the sound of Christine singing 'Wishing you were somehow here again' in *Phantom of the Opera* (Lloyd Webber, Hart and Stilgoe), then listen to Audrey singing 'Somewhere that's green' in *Little Shop of Horrors* (Ashman and Menken) and think about the differences of delivery, roughly equating to the difference between an operatic and a folk-rock sound. Or you might notice the difference between 'King Herod's song', sung by Herod, and 'Gethsemane', sung by Jesus, in *Jesus Christ Superstar* (Rice and Lloyd Webber) – the first is in a music-hall tradition, the second is in a pop-rock style. You could then relate the singing style to the characterization and look at the campness of Pilate and the authenticity of Jesus as partly determined by the qualities of their music and, consequently, their vocal delivery. Very quickly you become aware that musical theatre encompasses a wide range of styles. However, singing in a rock musical and singing in a rock concert are still different. The musical-theatre version of each style requires a strong focus on the words, the development of story and the representation of the character in comparison to a concert version of that style of singing.

So what are the various styles of singing that you might consider when preparing to sing in musical theatre?

Jazz

There are a number of types of jazz, but I want to focus here on two aspects of vocal delivery that are typified in different types of jazz performance and that are useful in musical-theatre singing. The first is the use of a breathy quality of the voice that requires close amplification so that, as a listener, you feel close to the singer, almost to the extent of feeling her breath on your face and her words whispering in your ear. There is a degree of intimacy about this style of singing, as the singer appears to be whispering sentimental phrases directly to you. This creates a personal delivery style and a close communication often of an emotional message. The words are

foregrounded, and the vocal range tends to be low and within the parameters of a sustained speech. The dynamic range is quiet, though the song will usually have an emotional and musical climax. The production values and the technology become audible as reverberation and other effects and the sound of the amplification can be discerned in both live and recorded performances. However, the sound of the voice, which is the primary concern here, is intimate, low in pitch and dynamic range, breathy and with clearly articulated words often in speech pattern rhythms.

The second area of jazz performance, which requires quite a different style of singing, is scat singing or improvisation. Here the music takes primacy as the voice becomes an instrument rather than the vehicle for the delivery of words and the communication of intimate breathy sounds. The tone becomes purer and the pitch range greater as the emotional level is more joyous and the performance level much larger, more extrovert, less intimate. This type of vocal performance feels as though it is addressed to a crowd at a concert, who will all enjoy the musical invention together and applaud the moments of ingenuity.

Opera

An operatic or classically trained sound is necessary for certain types of art music and particularly opera and operetta. There are some overlaps between musical theatre and operetta, and some singers who cross the boundaries between forms but, in general, a highly trained voice that can carry over orchestral forces has a particular placing of the vocal mechanism and focus in the body's resonators that distinguishes it from many other forms of singing. The tone of the voice will aim for the maximum purity and consistency. Whereas many forms of popular singing embrace the cracks and impurities of the voice as signs of authenticity and emotional truth, the operatic or classically trained voice focuses on fluidity, flexibility and a smooth tone throughout. Although opera singers generally articulate the words clearly and attempt to deliver an emotional characterization, the tone of the voice does not alter enormously in the expression of emotion, since the focus is on retaining a continuous and fluid sound over the vocal range. Rather, the musical language suggests the emotional shape of phrases, so the listener discovers the story and the emotions through melody and accompaniment. This is in contrast to musical theatre in which the singer will attempt to recreate the emotional landscape in the vocal colour, verbal attack and articulation, and resonance.

The characteristics of an operatic delivery then might be summarized as an extremely resonant and pure tone, a large pitch range, a focus on long, fluid musical lines, the ability to project in large auditoria over orchestral forces and the articulation of emotion through the musical accompaniment and melody, which are not merely the vehicles for the delivery of words.

Some singers manage to cross between styles more easily than others. Renée Fleming began as a jazz singer and moved into opera, and still, despite the operatic training, can reproduce the breathy qualities and intimate style of jazz. On the other hand, who can forget the nightmare José Carreras had when recording *West Side Story* conducted by Leonard Bernstein (broadcast by the BBC and released as a concert performance on CD)? It was not only Carreras' accent that Bernstein

objected to, but the rounded and beautiful sounds of the voice that impeded the verbal articulation and attack that are required for the characterization through voice.

Country, Folk and Rock

Whereas in opera the story is told through the musical journey that is amplified by the words, and by a beautiful voice, folk music is fundamentally about the delivery of words. Country music in the US developed from British and European folk music taken to America by immigrants. The important feature of that music is that it is part of a storytelling tradition in which the music is clearly the vehicle for words. Even though the musical structures are repetitive patterns of verse and chorus, and often repeated sentence structures with slight alterations, this merely serves to highlight the difference from verse to verse and so tell the story with the least possible means. Take for example, the verses of 'On Ilkley Moor Baht'At', which consist of only one changing line yet outline a sequence of events. The verses to 'Bobby Shaftoe' tell the story of courtship, childbirth and marriage (in that order) through partially repeated verbal patterns and completely repeated music. 'Widdicombe Fair' is another example.

The subject matter of country music, like that of folk music, is everyday life, so instead of songs about working in the fields, going to sea or going to the fair, more modern country songs speak of urban life and relationships. Examples speak of 'Working nine to five', the requirement to 'Stand by your man' or the breakdown of relationships in 'D-I-V-O-R-C-E'. The tone of the voice and the word setting are deliberately straightforward and relate to the pitches and rhythms of speech, while repeated choruses offer the opportunity for more elaborate musical improvisation without detracting from the development of the story or delivery of the punch-line. The significant addition to the sound of folk music that is apparent in country music, and particularly country rock music, is the introduction of the 'belt' voice. I will talk more about techniques for this style of delivery below, but its importance here is that it is a full-bodied sound. The listener feels that it is unconstrained, fully open and communicates the emotion of the body. It is the passionate nature of the sound that articulates the emotional expressivity of country music.

Country music singing has an enormous similarity to musical-theatre singing for both these reasons: that it uses clearly articulated words to share information and tell stories; that the vocal sound quality is extended to reveal and express the physical and emotional state of the singing body. Musical theatre can offer more complex characterizations, however, because the physical and emotional state revealed in the music and voice might be deliberately countered in the words, but more of this later. There are examples of country music in musical theatre in, for example, *The Best Little Whorehouse in Texas*, or in the use of particular characters as in *Starlight Express* in which Dinah sings the country song 'U-N-C-O-U-P-L-E-D' to express her situation and her origins.

Rock and roll and then rock music grew out of country music and the two are deeply entwined. However, the significant difference in voice production between the two centres on the importance of the words in country music and the use of a noise aesthetic to signify emotion in rock. The use of technology in all forms of popular music has allowed new types of voice production, so that quieter and lower parts of the voice can be heard (listen to Bing Crosby for an early example of the difference to voice production caused by the development of microphone technology). But in rock music, the ability to create distortion between sound source and amplifier, and the ability to express loud and extreme emotional sounds of the body coupled with electronic instruments, has led to an aesthetic where noise and loudness are perceived as synonymous with the authentic representation of emotion and the anger of alienation in a modern world. There is also a represented relationship with an urban and working class culture.

The difference between rock concerts and rock musicals is that musicals have stories and characters that must remain consistent throughout the performance, whereas rock concerts rely on the projected persona of the singer, who may sing many different songs in the course of the evening. Take, for example, *The Rocky Horror Show* (O'Brien), which consists of a series of songs interrupted by short scenes, but that have a consistent narrative and through which the fantastic characters are introduced and developed. In many ways the show feels like a rock concert as each new song is recognized and enjoyed by the audience, as the guitar riffs and drum breaks vibrate through the auditorium and reverberate in the bodies of the audience, and as the audience leaps up to join in 'The time warp'. However, the effectiveness of 'I'm going home' is made possible by the relationship the audience has developed with the character Frank, not simply by the song alone.

Musicals
The result of this is that, although musical-theatre singers need to be able to use a range of

vocal sounds to deliver some of the qualities of jazz, some of the range and technique of opera and some of the noise and aggression of rock, the key feature that unifies voice production in musical theatre is that the story is told, the characters are developed and the emotions are shared through song. This means that the singer must clearly articulate the words, must understand the song structure and its place in the story (what it is saying musically as well as verbally), and that he/she must be able to re-create the emotional qualities of the situation using all the sounds of the voice, not just the beautiful ones.

So take that breath in again and release it on an 'Aah'. Listen to the sound you're making and then move the sound around, open and close your mouth, move the sound into your nose. All these sounds are different, and they're all useful when you're trying to create a character's sound and her/his emotional world. So you CAN sing, but you may need to learn to listen and to feel your sound much more closely, and to analyse and control what is happening in your body. Then you will be able to create and reproduce the sounds you want to make and the sounds that are effective in the situations and for the characters in the musical of your choice.

WORKING THROUGH THIS BOOK

The book is arranged in two parts: the first part contains a chapter on the physiology of the vocal mechanism followed by exercises to develop your body and voice ready for singing songs; the second part gives a brief survey of the development of musical theatre with a particular focus on the development of vocal style, before separate chapters that discuss how you

might prepare particular types of song for performance. The first chapter in each part is essential to your general understanding, but need not be read before proceeding to the other chapters. The information contained in these chapters is necessary in order to develop, but you may want to study them gradually alongside your progress through the other parts of the book.

The learning is incremental in both parts of the book, but relies on your increasing awareness of your own sound and your own needs, so that you can pick exercises and challenges to develop your own technique. So, for example, if you are a relative beginner, I would suggest you work slowly through all the exercises in the early chapters before even looking at the second half of the book. If you are an experienced performer, you might look at the relaxation and vocal development exercises as an *aide-mémoire* or a tool for analysing your own vocal technique and as a stimulus for further development, while also working on songs in the ways suggested in the second part. I have tried always to explain why an exercise is important and what it is for, so that you could replace it with another similar exercise that you prefer, or adapt it for variety without losing its efficacy. Finally, you might want to work with a partner or group occasionally or frequently to get feedback on your development, but this is for you to decide as you feel confident.

What you should end up with at the end of Part 1 is a series of exercises drawn from those suggested or developed according to the purpose of the exercise as identified that suit your voice and work as a warm-up for you. You should also have identified a programme of areas for improvement in your voice for which, after working through the suggested exercises, you pick and choose exercises from the vocal development sections. I would suggest that you also work through all of the second part of the book, looking at the scores of the songs so that you understand the points being made even if the song is not suitable for you. However, there are suggestions of songs within certain categories, so try to find songs that are suitable for you within each category, so that you extend the type of songs and styles in which you are able to perform. Then you can apply the ideas and techniques suggested to any song you need to perform as appropriate to the effects you are trying to create.

What this book aims to do is to give you the awareness of your own voice and body, so that you understand what is happening to your sound, how you are making particular sounds and why you might choose to create particular effects. The object of all this is to empower you to be able to sing in a range of styles, respond to direction in a positive way, and work consistently to improve and be excited by the possibilities of expressing character and emotion through musical theatre songs.

PART 1

DEVELOPING YOUR VOICE

1 PHYSIOLOGY

As said in the Introduction, the information contained in this chapter is essential to understanding of your voice and, therefore, to your ability to develop it without damage. However, you need not read this chapter first, but read it alongside your practice of the exercises in the following chapters.

Although there is a common misconception that there are different 'voices', a chest voice, a head voice and so on, these perceptions are drawn from two features of vocal technique. These are, firstly, that the skeletal structures of many parts of the body vibrate as a result of the resonance of the voice, which is itself produced by vibration; secondly, that singers have the ability to alter the quality of the voice so that it appears to be rounder and more mellow, or sharper and more attacking, and so on. We all do this all the time, whispering softly and breathily into the ear of a lover, or barking an order to stop a child running into the road. We understand the emotions projected into an angry voice or a passionate voice. The purpose of any singing technique is to become aware of the physical processes by which sounds are projected so that they can be repeated at will, without danger to the voice.

In rehearsal for Robinson Crusoe at the Yvonne Arnaud Theatre, Guildford, in 1990.

The Production of Sound

There are four stages to the production of vocal and verbal sound:

(1) the supply of air through inhalation and exhalation to the vocal cords (folds), supported by the muscles of the torso
(2) the creation of sound as the air passes through the vocal folds – the folds create pressure against the airflow and vibrate at varying speeds and in different ways to create sounds
(3) the amplification of the sound, which can be altered by the adaptation of the shape of the laryngeal tube and by the direction of the sound into the resonating cavities of the mouth and nose
(4) the articulation of that sound into words by the muscles of the tongue, mouth and lips.

INHALATION AND EXHALATION – BREATHING

To supply sufficient air for singing is not a difficult task, it's something we accomplish throughout our lives for speaking, shouting and for all physical activities. However, singing requires a relaxed control of the physiology so that sufficient air is available for the task concerned.

In the course of breathing and speaking, air flows into the body from the mouth and nose, down past the pharynx, larynx and trachea, and separates into the two bronchial tubes and into the two spongy masses of the lungs. These fill with air, which can then be sent back to create pressure on the vocal folds, which open sufficiently to create vibrations as the air passes back between them. The vibrating air, and consequently the sound, is then directed to the resonators and articulators. However, for singing, the body sometimes needs more air, more sustained exhalation and greater effort than for speaking. This effort comes from the musculature of the torso.

The twelve ribs attached to the spine create a protective cavern for the lungs. The upper seven ribs are attached at the front to the sternum or breastbone. The next three ribs are attached to each other by cartilage. The final two ribs are described as 'floating', as they are not attached at the front. This area of the body is encased in muscles that assist in the expansion and contraction of the thorax as air is inhaled and exhaled. The external intercostals run diagonally from the side of the body and down to the front of the body, joining one rib to the next one down. They assist in pulling the ribs to the side, back and up as the lungs are filled with air, increasing the size of the lung cavity. There are several other muscle groups that assist in this work when larger inhalations are required. The internal intercostals do the opposite, pulling the ribs back in and down for exhalation, but are assisted to a greater

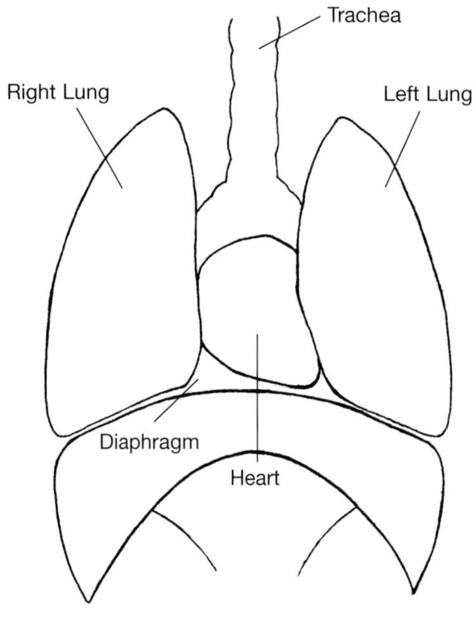

Figure 1 – Lungs and trachea.

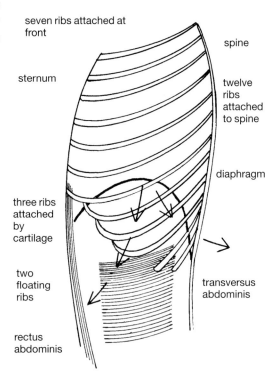

Figure 2 - The ribs.

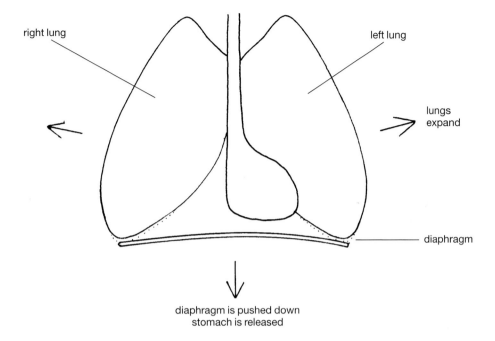

right lung

left lung

lungs expand

diaphragm

diaphragm is pushed down
stomach is released

Figure 3 – Breathing in – inhalation.

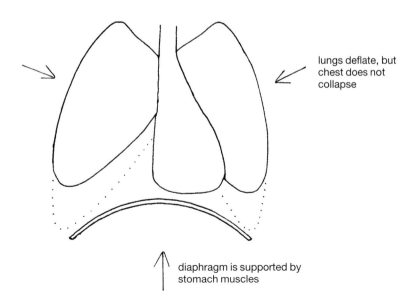

lungs deflate, but
chest does not
collapse

diaphragm is supported by
stomach muscles

Figure 4 – Breathing out – exhalation.

extent by the abdominal muscles: transverses abdominis and rectus abdominis.

The lungs themselves have an enormous range. From their neutral position they can expand, but equally, in longer phrases, they can contract beyond the neutral position squeezing more air out. After exhalation, a vacuum is created into which air is sucked; this is the most efficient inhalation method as it relies on the body's own instinctive mechanisms and means that you will never have to worry about taking in air.

The diaphragm is a muscle that separates the heart and lungs (the thorax) from the stomach and digestive system and other organs (the abdomen). It is like a large, upturned bowl fastened to the sternum (breastbone), ribs and spine. If you cough gently, with a hand resting just above your belly button, you will feel it kick. When the lungs fill with air, the diaphragm flattens and pushes downwards. This increases the size of the lung cavity, but decreases the room in the abdomen, which has to release outwards in turn, pushing the stomach out. During exhalation the abdominal muscles push back in so that the diaphragm releases back upwards contracting the space in the lungs and pushing the air out to the vocal folds.

The reason for this long explanation is to preface some instructions.

- Don't wear a tightly fastened belt or otherwise constrict your abdomen when singing. Although it may not be fashionable, you need to allow your stomach to release out on an in-breath and you need the strength of your abdominal muscles to assist the exhalation.
- Breathing is a natural activity – you don't need to control it in order to sing (though for some phrases and styles you may choose to), but there are some things you will need to practise and sensations you will need to get used to. There are some exercises in Chapter 5 for inhalation and controlled exhalation.
- Support for singing comes from the muscles of the torso, but is only needed for certain styles of singing and qualities of vocal tone. When effort is needed, it will come from these muscles. The rest of the body needs to stay released.

PHONATION – CREATING SOUND

The vocal folds or cords (the words are commonly used interchangeably) are not actually cords at all, but a flat muscle across the airway with a split in the middle that can open and close with enormous agility and delicacy. They are situated across the larynx and, when closed, block the airway. Though the epiglottis also blocks the airway, its purpose is to prevent food entering the airway, while the vocal folds open and close for the protection of the airway, as well as the production of sound.

Vocal sound is created by air passing through the partially closed vocal cords or folds. The pressure of the compressed air as it is forced through the narrow channel between the folds causes the folds and the air to vibrate. Just like the strings of a violin or a guitar, or the reed of an oboe, the vibration of the cords and the movement of the surrounding air produces a small sound. This is amplified by the throat and mouth just as the violin or guitar sound is amplified by the body of the instrument.

Amplification or resonance will be explained fully below.

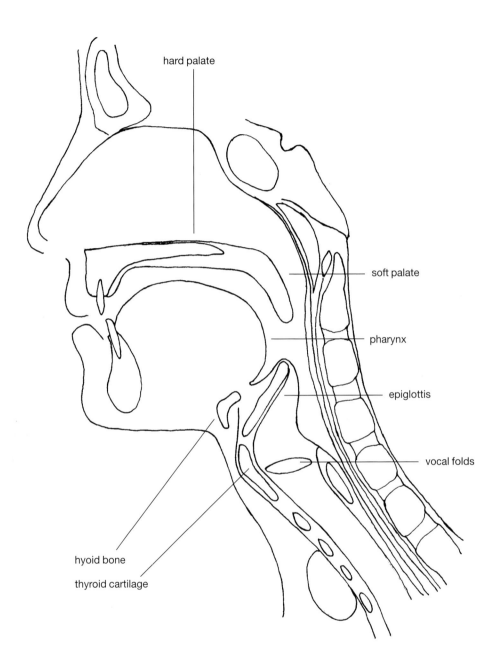

Figure 5 – Position of vocal mechanism in upper body.

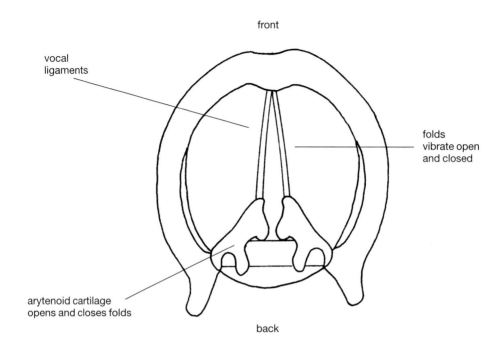

Figure 6 – Vocal folds from above.

The vocal folds open for air to be taken in, then they close. The air is pushed back out through the folds with the energy of the diaphragm and the muscles of the torso. The folds open to varying degrees for different pitches and intensities. The pressure of air can vary, depending on the amount of energy with which the air is exhaled and, if the vocal folds are open, there need be no sound. However, the vocal folds can close a little or a lot, and the smaller the gap for the air to be pushed through and the greater the energy of the exhalation, the greater the resistance. It is a combination of the energy of the breath and the resistance of the vocal cords that creates the sound and varies its force, pitch and intensity.

The vocal cords are protected by two cartilages, which you can feel as the hard protrusion in the neck and which, in men, develops into the Adam's Apple. The thyroid cartilage is the upper section, which is attached to the cricoid cartilage by a hinged joint as shown in the diagram on page 23.

These two cartilages protect the vocal mechanism but, since the whole mechanism is cartilage and muscle, it is not fixed. This means that the movement of the cricoid in relation to the thyroid cartilage at the hinged joint can stretch or reduce the length of the vocal folds. There is a range of muscles that assist the movement of these cartilages, which are unnecessary to mention here, but you can find more information about them if you are interested in Meribeth Bunch's book *The Dynamics of the Singing Voice* listed in the reference section. The vocal mechanism is suspended from the hyoid bone, so that the

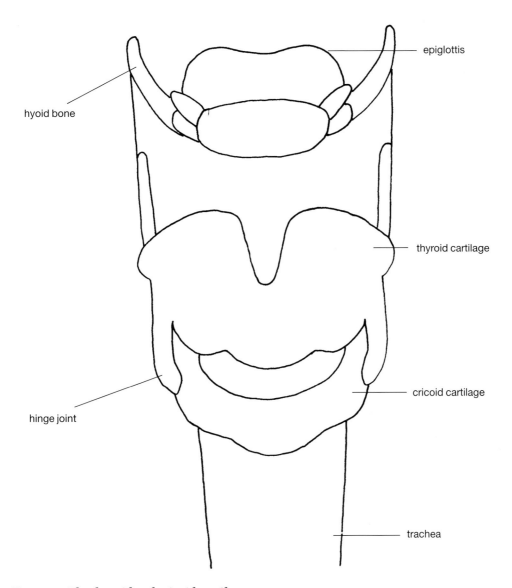

epiglottis

hyoid bone

thyroid cartilage

cricoid cartilage

hinge joint

trachea

Figure 7 – The thyroid and cricoid cartilages.

whole mechanism is quite mobile, suspended by muscle within a system of muscles and cartilages. This is important because the mobility allows the variety of sounds that singing requires.

The variety of sound qualities and pitches required for speaking and singing relies on the fine-tuning of the thickness of the cords, their stretch or relaxation and the amount of space between them at any given time. But the folds do not simply open and close uniformly along their length. They close at some parts along

23

their length, leaving a small gap through which air passes and which section vibrates, or the folds themselves become thicker or finer to alter the quality of the sound. In general, just like stringed instruments, the shorter the vibrating section of the fold, the higher the pitch of the sound, but the thickness of the string or fold also affects quality. These variations can be seen in some videos, such as *The Dynamics of the Singing Voice,* published by the Voice Foundation in 1987, which shows the changes in the folds and in the laryngeal and pharyngeal position as a singer moves through a range of pitches.

It is not necessary to know what is happening to your vocal folds at particular moments in singing, because the operation of the folds happens automatically when you decide to make particular sounds. However, it does help to be aware of the extremely fine and detailed mechanism of the voice: firstly, so that you treat it with care; secondly, so that you understand that, like all muscles, it needs regular, gentle practice rather than being over-used one day and then abandoned for a week; thirdly, understanding the operation of the vocal mechanism will help you to be aware of the way tension in one part of the body affects other parts; and, finally, you will be more able to identify sources of constriction and tension if you understand how the voice works.

RESONANCE – AMPLIFYING THE SOUND

As mentioned above, the small sound produced by the vocal folds requires amplification. This happens in the larynx itself, in the pharynx and, most importantly, in the mouth. The larynx and pharynx are mobile and have soft

Looking After Your Voice

Like all muscles, the vocal cords and all the associated muscles need regular stretching and development in order to increase their flexibility and agility. If you are going to run a marathon, you run regularly over the course of several months and gradually increase the distance you are able to run and the pace you can maintain. If you haven't run for several months and suddenly attempt to run a long distance, the muscles become stiff and tired and can react with soreness or injury. You need to think of the vocal muscles in the same way. They respond to regular, gentle practice to increase their mobility, and the range of pitch and sound quality that you can achieve.

surfaces, therefore, although they do act as resonators and have an effect on the quality of the sound, they are not efficient resonators. The base of the tongue can affect resonance in two ways: by interfering with the direction of the vibrating air and interrupting its flow to the resonance of the hard palate; since it is connected to the muscles of the larynx, any tension in the tongue also affects the sound production in the vocal mechanism.

The most effective resonator is the hard palate or roof of the mouth, which, being made of bone provides a hard surface from which the vibrations can rebound. Resonation also occurs in the nasal cavities if the sound is directed there. Vibrations also pass through the palate into the other bones and cavities of the skull. These are not actually resonators, rather they vibrate in sympathy. For this reason, many people have the sensation that resonation occurs in the face, the skull or the

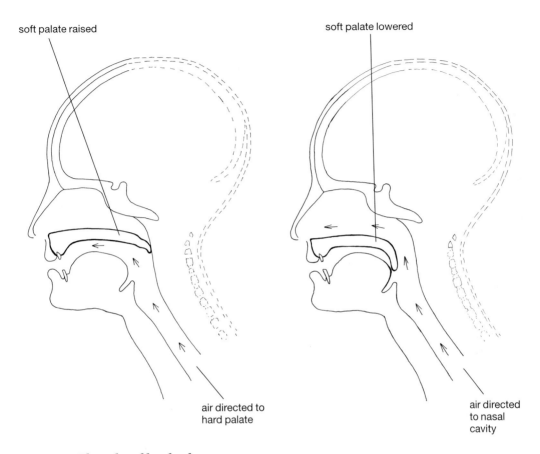

soft palate raised

soft palate lowered

air directed to
hard palate

air directed
to nasal
cavity

Figure 8 – The soft and hard palates.

head, as well as the throat, neck and chest. Vibration occurs in all these places, but the resonance that amplifies the sound occurs in the mouth or nasal cavities.

The sound needs to be directed efficiently to the hard palate by the shaping of the larynx, pharynx and the tongue, according to the vowel shapes described below. The soft palate is a flap of muscle at the back of the mouth that directs the airflow either into the nasal passages or into the mouth. For the majority of singing, the soft palate needs to be raised so that the air flows to the hard palate. One way of getting the sensation of this is to yawn and feel the stretch at the back of the mouth. This lifted sensation is useful for the direction of sound, but also when attempting to increase range. However, there are certain times when you might choose to use a nasal sound, or to mix some nasal sound with oral resonance, and there are some sounds that can only be created using nasal resonance. A nasal sound is sharp and piercing, but it carries well, so it can be useful in some circumstances. However, it is not a pleasant sound and so should be used sparingly.

To discover whether you are using nasal or oral resonance you can try the following exercises. Sing 'ng', deliberately sending the sound through the nose. In order to do this, you have to lower the soft palate and use the resonance of the nasal cavities. Put your hand in front of your mouth and then your nose to feel where the breath is coming from. It should be coming from your nose. Now sing an open 'ee' sound and feel the outflow of breath from the mouth. The 'ee' sound is the closest vowel to the 'ng' sound because the tongue is raised at the back. Now move between 'ee' and 'ng' and feel the movement in the back of the mouth as the soft palate rises to send vibrations into the mouth, or lowers to send vibrations into the nasal cavities. This is assisted by a movement of the back of the tongue.

Listen to the difference in sound quality you can produce by this movement. On most occasions you will achieve the most aesthetically pleasing sound by using the oral resonators, but for certain consonants and for certain sound qualities you need to mix the sound or use nasal resonance. You need to practise creating resonance in both ways, but especially concentrating on the feeling of creating a resonant sound on the hard palate of the mouth.

ARTICULATION – SHAPING THE SOUND

Already, in exploring the movement of tongue and soft palate to create resonance, you will have discovered how important the shape of the mouth is in directing the flow of air to the hard palate. Each vowel shape requires a position of the tongue and mouth that shapes the sound effectively, while maximizing the resonance. The following are five examples, but practising all the vowel sounds listed in the

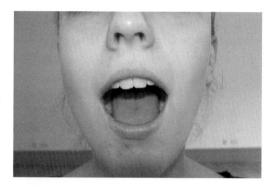

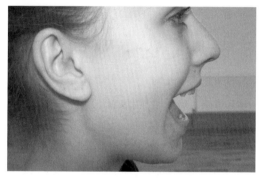

Mouth shape for 'ah' as in Cart.

table below will allow you to begin to understand the different vocal shapes required. At the same time listen to the resonance of each sound and make sure that the airflow is being directed to the hard palate and the resonance is creating a vibrant tone.

Although written English has only five vowels, there are eleven sung single vowels and six compound vowels or diphthongs. A diphthong is written as a vowel but produced vocally by the combination of two of the simple vowels.

You can create exercises by putting together groups of up to five of the single vowel sounds, with or without a consonant in front, and practising them on one note. This allows the clarity of the vowel sounds and the placement of the tongue in each vowel to be practised. More information about the articulation of diphthongs will be included later, but for now,

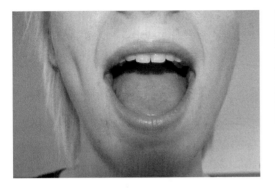

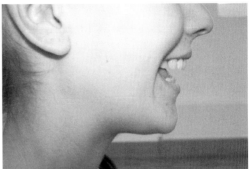

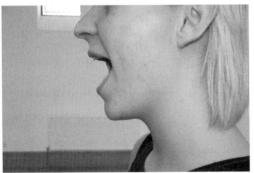

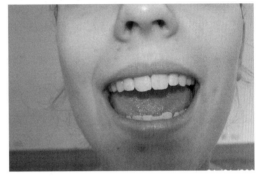

Mouth shape for 'eh' as in Get.

Mouth shape for 'ee' as in Lee.

Vowels and Diphthongs		
ee	as in	Lee
i	as in	Hid
e	as in	Get
a	as in	Cat
er	as in	Turn
u	as in	But
ah	as in	Cart
o	as in	Bob
aw	as in	Fall
oo	as in	Look
oo	as in	Room
ee-oo (u)	as in	Fume
eh-ee (ay)	as in	Lake
ah-ee (i)	as in	Mike
ah-oo (ou)	as in	Doubt
aw-ee (oi)	as in	Boil
oh-oo (o)	as in	Tone

practise singing on the first of the two vowels listed above and then switching cleanly to the second vowel at the last moment before the consonant.

Consonants can be grouped as follows:

- p, b and m are formed between the upper and lower lips
- f and v are formed between the lower lip and upper teeth
- w is formed by the upper and lower lips with the back of the tongue raised
- th (as in thin) and the darker th (as in this) are formed by the tip of the tongue and the upper teeth
- t, d, s, z, l and n are all formed by the tip of the tongue and the ridge of the hard palate behind the upper teeth

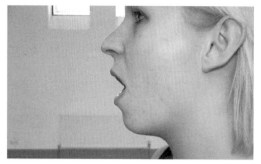

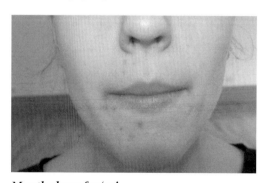

Mouth shape for 'o' as in Mob.

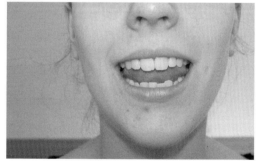

Mouth shape for 'oo' as in Room.

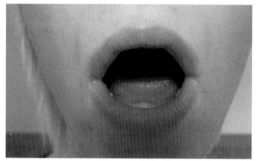

Mouth shape for 'f'.

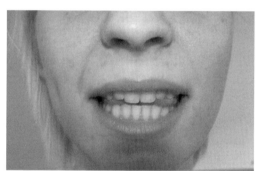

Mouth shape for 't'.

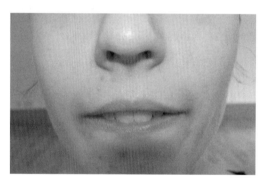

Mouth shape for 'm'.

Mouth shape for 'l'.

- sh, ge, j, ch and, to some extent, r are formed between the tongue and the hard palate slightly behind the ridge
- y is formed between the middle of the tongue and the hard palate
- k, g and ng are formed between the back of the tongue and the soft palate
- h and the glottal before a vowel are formed between the vocal folds.

The majority of singing practice takes place using vowels, as the open sounds create the greatest resonance. However, since the purpose of most singing in musicals is the communication of verbal ideas in song, it is important that clear articulation takes place. Therefore you will need to practise vowels so that each vowel shape is comfortable, reliable and resonant. Then practise placing each consonant before and after each vowel until the movements of the tongue, lips and mouth are dynamic and clear. There are exercises to improve articulation in the chapters below, but for now it is important to become familiar with the shapes and patterns of the mouth, and to be able to articulate clearly without creating tension in the jaw, face or tongue.

As you will be aware from the explanations above, all the parts of the vocal mechanism are linked by muscles so that tension in one part of the mechanism easily affects sound quality, not only at the source of the tension, but tension in one part can affect the efficiency of other parts of the musculature. The body-release exercises that follow are particularly important in beginning to identify and release such sources of tension, but it is important in all the exercises and songs that you practise, that you remain aware of tension as a constriction to efficient and effective sound production.

2 RELEASING THE BODY

The exercises contained in this chapter should be worked through in order, on a number of occasions, so that you understand the effect of the release of tension on your voice. Gradually you might refine the number of exercises you use on each occasion, but you will always need to incorporate some of these exercises into your warm-up. It is also helpful to work through this process as a reminder to your body of where tension lies and how to release it at regular intervals. You should attempt to become much more aware of how you hold your body throughout your everyday life, releasing tension as much as possible for efficient functioning in all activities.

There are several different types of exercises that include stretching, swinging, dropping and shaking. In stretching exercises stretch until you begin to feel the muscle but do not push or bounce. Just like in yoga, the idea is to feel the extension but not to cause pain. Hold the extension and breathe into the stretch concentrating on releasing the muscles so that they extend further. Other exercises require that you shake a part of the body, again so that any muscles that are being held are released. This is also a useful antidote to a more strenuous exercise. Yet others rely on swinging in a

relaxed manner, which has the same effect as shaking, but tends to allow the body to go further than it would generally go. Swings should therefore not be performed at the beginning of the session, but when the body is warmer. Finally, dropping exercises (which are mostly included in the next chapter) rely on the ability to hold a position and suddenly release the muscles, and should also be performed only when warm. These exercises allow you to see how much tension you are really holding as it becomes almost a struggle with the mind to let a part of the body fall.

Some exercises focus on particular parts of the body and others use the whole body, some are lying on the floor so that the body is supported, others are standing and require balance (and thus a little more tension). The face-massage exercises can be performed sitting, lying or standing. However, the common factor is that the exercises are designed to release as much unnecessary tension as possible from wherever it is held in your body to prepare the body to sing.

The greatest impediment to a free sound is unwanted and unnecessary tension. In order to sing efficiently, to produce the greatest range of sounds and to know how to reproduce different parts of your vocal range at will, you need to become much more aware of your body and release the tensions you hold. Notice that I mention releasing tension rather than relaxation. The body needs to use and direct energy in order to stand or move, and it requires considerable energy in the breath to sing in a sustained or dynamic way. The important point is that unnecessary tension also requires energy to sustain it, and misusing energy detracts from your total available energy, so that you are less able to produce sound and will tire more easily. Also unnecessary tension is likely to constrict parts of the body that need to be free and supportive of your singing mechanism.

The exercises outlined below will draw on many techniques, which are adapted to focus on release of the body for singing. You will need to be in a warm room, with a mat on the floor to lie on, and you will need to dress in loose comfortable clothing, a track suit or a leotard, so that you can move your body and your limbs without constriction. Try all these exercises and make note of the effect that this release has on the voice. However, you will not always have the time or space to perform all these exercises. So, once you are comfortable with all the exercises, you need to choose those that are most effective for you, and to develop a short and a long sequence of exercises that you can use as time and space allow, perhaps performing the short sequence daily and as part of a warm-up, and the long sequence once or twice a week before a longer vocal development session.

FLOOR WORK

Lying Down

First, sit on the floor with your knees drawn up, your feet flat on the floor at hip-width apart and your hands gently placed around your knees. Keep your head and eyes down and your back curved forward, but don't round your shoulders from the sides. Slowly roll your back down onto the floor, vertebra by vertebra, leaving your chin on your chest until last. Finally, release the weight of your head onto the floor. Drop your hands onto your hips and let your elbows reach out to each side of you. Your knees should still be raised, with your feet flat on the floor at hip-width apart. You may find that you need to pull your feet slightly closer to your body after having rolled down.

Now examine your body for tension. Begin by exploring the arch in your back. There is a natural curvature in the spine that absorbs shock and impact. This should remain so that

---

Releasing Tension

There are many techniques for releasing tension and being much more aware of body use, including the Alexander technique, yoga, Feldenkreis and pilates. Not surprisingly, there are similarities between them, since there is an optimum way of using your body that all of these techniques attempt to stimulate awareness of. So if you have studied any of them you will already be on your way to making the best use of your body. However, there are also subtle differences that you need to be aware of. For example, pilates encourages breathing without release of the stomach, which is essential to vocal support. The most important task at this point in your development is to start to become aware of your own body, its shapes, its habitual patterns and its tensions.

Lying down.

you can slide a hand underneath the middle of your back. Think about your neck, which, after having rolled down, should be extended from your shoulders and, since it is no longer supporting your head, holding no tension. Register your breath and feel your stomach rising and falling as you take breath into and out of your body. Think about your hips and legs and make sure you are not holding tight with your muscles, but that your knees feel as though they are balanced with energy rising from them to the ceiling. Now turn your attention to your shoulders and feel the weight of your shoulders releasing any habitual tension that holds your shoulders either forward or upwards. Let your shoulders release so that you have the sensation of your shoulders being drawn out to either side of you. Your

elbows, too, are being drawn away to either side. Finally think about your face and neck, your jaw and the base of your tongue. Make sure you are not clenching your teeth or holding your jaw, and become aware of your tongue lying calmly on the floor of your mouth.

This position is a useful starting point for releasing tension, but can also be used for many of the breathing and sounding exercises in the following chapters.

Stretching Out

Stretch one arm up into the air until you have lifted the shoulder off the floor. Hold for a couple of seconds, before returning the shoulder and then the arm to the floor. Feel how the shoulder rolls back down and that side of the

Lift the shoulder.

body has expanded out to the side. Do the same with the other arm and shoulder.

Raise one knee to the chest, gently feeling the stretch of the lower back before rolling the hip and leg back down. Feel how the back has lengthened. Do the same with the other leg.

With both feet on the floor, raise the hips and pelvis to the ceiling, don't push, just gently raise, hold for a couple of seconds and lower, feeling any changes to the length of the back and the curvature of the spine.

Shaking Out

In exactly the same sequence, raise one arm to the ceiling, but this time when the arm is extended shake it so that it is relaxed and floppy. Let the shoulder join in with the feeling of being shaken as much as possible before

33

Extending the lower back.

lowering the arm again, and extending the elbow to the side. Do the same with the other arm. Extend your leg out until it is almost straight and at a height that is comfortable for you (probably about a foot or so off the ground). Shake the leg out, feeling the release in the hip joint before returning the leg to its starting position. Repeat on the other side. Finally raise the pelvis and shake the lower body up and down and from side to side. Return to your starting position and register the feeling of extension and release in your body. Check for signs of tension and consciously release them.

Leg Swinging

This exercise is designed to release tension in the abdomen and to release the hips and lower back ready for breathing exercises later. It can be done standing at a bar or in an open space,

but requires more energy and control to balance, so is best worked on the floor, at least at first.

Open the arms out at shoulder length and lengthen the legs out flat onto the floor. Feel the back lengthening and extending out from head and feet and to the sides through the fingers extended at each side. Gently and slowly, and with your arms, head and shoulders remaining on the floor, swing the right leg over the left leg until it is at about knee height (the crossed position). Turning the head away from the knee increases the stretch in the back.

Then bend the knee and continue to raise the leg as far as is comfortable. Swing the leg back to the starting point and then, allowing the knee to bend, raise the leg on the other side (the open position). Gently repeat the pendulum movement with this leg four or five times.

The crossed position.

The open position.

Releasing the shoulders.

Rolled to one side.

Now repeat with the other leg.

You can do a similar exercise with the arms, keeping the hips on the floor, but allowing the shoulders and head to join in the movement of each arm down past the legs and up to shoulder height across the body, and returning to the open position at shoulder height on its own side of the body. This exercise can also be done with the standing exercises, if preferred.

Rolling

Return to the start position with knees raised and feet flat on the ground, but with arms outstretched. Take the right arm in a semi-circle up to

Rolling the whole body.

Preparing to get up.

the ceiling and over to clap the left hand. But this time, allow the entire body to roll with the arm. The knees will curl into the body and fall over to the left and you will be lying in a foetal position on your left side with your arms outstretched.

Beginning the impulse with your arms, roll over to your right side. Repeat this several times, allowing your whole back to curve and release, and the contact with the floor to massage your back.

Getting Up

As you become comfortable with the rolling exercise you will build up the ability to use the

37

Crawling position – neck extended.

momentum to propel yourself up onto all fours, but for now roll gently onto your right side, then onto your right haunch, and push yourself up onto your knees with your back straight and your neck long.

Throughout all the rolling, maintain an awareness of the relationship of the head and neck to the body and, when you move onto all fours, retain this relationship. Do not let the head either fall forward or pull back into the shoulders.

Stop when you are on all fours and shake out your body, then your head, making sure that your head lengthens out of the spine (note that in the picture above the students have maintained the extension of the head rather than contracting the neck muscles to look up). Sit back on your haunches with your arms by your sides and your head rising above your shoulders. Now, lifting forward and up

with the top of your head, raise one leg so that the foot is flat on the floor and ascend into a standing position.

STANDING

Check your body for tension. In particular, check the feeling of elevation through your spine, and feel that your head is floating above your neck suspended on a piece of string. Make sure you haven't tightened your neck or your jaw. Stand with your feet apart, at about the width of your hips, and the knees slightly bent (i.e. not locked tight, but comfortably released). Feel that your shoulders are extending out to either side of you, and your chest is open.

There are two axes running through your body: a vertical axis running down from a string above your head, through the middle of

Sequence of poses during getting up.

Standing in Alignment

Have someone check your alignment from the front and the side. Your ears should be above your shoulders, which should be above your hips, which should be above the arches of your feet. Misalignments begin if the hips are too far forward or back, which leads to over arching of the back, compensatory positioning forward or back at the shoulders to maintain balance. This means that the neck and chin are angled and jut out or fall forcing tension into the neck and jaw muscles. From the front ask your friend to check that your hips and shoulders are at equal heights and your head is not leaning to one side. It may feel unnatural at first to stand correctly, which is why you need a friend to help you get used to an aligned position.

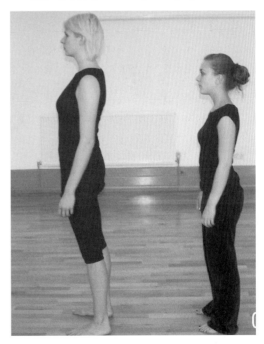

Standing in alignment.

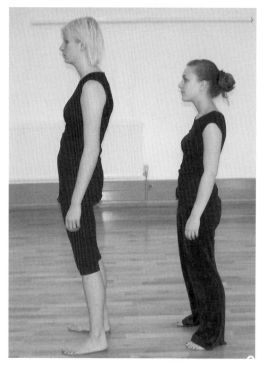

Examples of poor posture and unnecessary tension.

your head and down through your body into the ground; the horizontal axis is at the level of your shoulders and draws your body to its perfect width.

Swinging

Keeping your feet in place and your knees slightly bent, turn your whole body to face the right by spinning on the vertical axis. Now swing back to face the left. Find a gentle pace to keep swinging from one side to the other on the vertical axis. Notice how your arms, if left free, set up their own swinging pattern. Increase the energy and pace of the swing in the body until the arms swing out to shoulder height and fall around your body at the end of each turn. Slow down and return to a standing position. This provides you with a comfortable, correctly aligned and energized basic position for singing.

Neck Drops

To make sure your neck remains free, drop your chin onto your chest, without dropping your shoulders forward. Now, very slowly and gently roll your head so that your right ear is over your right shoulder and you are facing forward. Feel the stretch in the muscles at the left side of the neck. Relax in that position for about thirty seconds. Now roll the head back to the centre and round to the left hand side. Hold again and return to the centre. Do not do this exercise fast, though you can increase the speed and swing from side to side if your neck muscles feel loose, but do not roll your head all the way round in a circle.

Releasing the neck.

Hanging from the hips.

Swinging and hanging.

You can use the weight of your arm to increase the stretch. With your head dropped over your right shoulder reach over with your right hand so that your fingers just reach your left ear. Don't pull down but allow the weight of gravity to gently release the neck muscles. Check that there is no tension in your shoulders and breathe into the stretch.

Rolling Down

Drop your chin onto your chest again, then allow the vertebrae in the back to slowly follow, curling down slowly until you are hanging from the hips with your knees slightly bent. Keep your weight in the centre of your feet – don't allow your weight to fall back over your heels or forward over your toes. Feel the stretch in your neck and the release in your back.

Gently swing around your vertical axis – not from side-to-side – feeling the additional stretch and the release of tension. When you are ready, come to a stop and slowly uncurl by building one vertebra on the other until you are standing with your chin on your chest. Raise your head to its suspended position and check your shoulders are extended to the sides.

Side Stretches

With your feet placed a little wider apart, take the right arm up to the ceiling, next to your right ear. Gently lean over towards your left side keeping your hips in position. Do not allow your body to twist either forwards or backwards. The amount of movement you can achieve without twisting is quite small, so do not push too far, simply feel the stretch and return to the centre, lower your arm and repeat on the other side. If you have trouble with this exercise, include it in the lying down section as you will not be able to twist your body when lying down.

41

Stretching the waist and upper body muscles.

THE FACE, NECK AND JAW

Massaging the Face
Massage parts of your face and head in tiny circles with both hands at the same time. Begin at the back of the head by massaging the edge of the scalp where the head joins the neck, and gradually move around, following the edge of the bone, to the back of the ears. Then move around and put your thumbs under the chin, with the fingers on the cheek bones. Massage below the jaw with the thumbs while keeping the fingers still, then keep the thumbs still while you massage the cheeks and chin with the fingers. Move the fingers up to find the hollow in front of the ears

where the jaw connects to the skull. Allow the mouth to release during this massage – don't try to keep your mouth closed. Now massage across your top lip. So that nothing is left out, run your fingers up either side of your nose to your eyebrows and circle the bones above your eyes on the inside edge of the bone, before running up your temples to your forehead, and drawing the fingers outward from centre to side in the middle of the forehead.

Finally, allow the muscles to work for themselves. Open the mouth as wide as you can, so that the whole face is involved in an extended gesture of surprise and delight. Notice how all the muscles of the face are involved as eyebrows lift, eyes open, mouth opens wide and cheeks lift.

Then scrunch the face into a tight 'ooh' of distaste and feel the eyes tighten, lips pout forward and possibly curve down at the sides and cheeks lift. Practise these exaggerated expressions of surprise and distaste several times, holding each for about five seconds. Then relax and feel how alive and dynamic your face feels.

The Jaw

You have already begun to explore the release of the jaw by massaging the face, and with the surprise/distaste exercise above. The jaw connects to the skull in front of the ears, and if you place your fingers there you can feel the movements of the muscles and bones as you open and close your mouth. Now for a big stretch, stretch your arms up over your head, open your mouth and yawn as widely as you can. Repeat a number of times, feeling the movement of your jaw, and the expansion in the back of the mouth and top of the throat; we will return to this later.

One more exercise, developed from a yoga exercise: Drop the jaw open so that it feels that it is reaching down onto the chest. Slowly lower the head backwards feeling the stretch under your chin and in your facial muscles. Your mouth should be wide open to the ceiling, as though ready to catch a raindrop. Now gently close the jaw feeling the stretch in the chin and neck, before returning the head to the upright position. Incidentally, this is also recommended to improve the appearance of double chins and dropping jowls. Notice the feeling of stretch in the chin and neck muscles, the lightness of the head and the release of the jaw, whether or not the lips are closed.

The Tongue

We will return to the tongue later for a series of articulation exercises, but first, you need to be sure you are aware when you are holding tension in the tongue. Some people really dislike this exercise because they think they look bad and because they feel rude sticking their tongue out. However, it is a useful exercise, so if you are worried, do this one in private.

Open your mouth as much as necessary to extend the tongue so that it is pointing out in front of you. Hold for five seconds before pointing the tongue to the right for five seconds, to the left for five seconds, up to the ceiling for five seconds, and down to the ground for five seconds. Finally point it out in front again for another five seconds before releasing. You will feel the muscles complaining before you get through this exercise, but persevere, because the release when you finish allows you to become much more aware of tension at the base of the tongue.

For exercising the middle of the tongue, place the tip of the tongue behind the lower teeth, then open the mouth as much as necessary to push the middle of the tongue up so that it curls forward and out of the mouth. Make small movements with the middle of the tongue by pressing against the teeth and trying to extend the tongue forward. This feels most peculiar, but again makes you aware of the different parts of your tongue.

Finally for the front of the tongue, begin by licking your lips, running the tongue over top and bottom lips in a circle first to the right and then to the left. Run the tongue around the teeth on the inside and the outside. Then poke the tongue very delicately into all the extremes of the mouth, feeling the different shapes of your teeth, the floor of the mouth, and the sides and back of your mouth.

One more yawn to stretch your face out and relax.

You should now feel that your body and

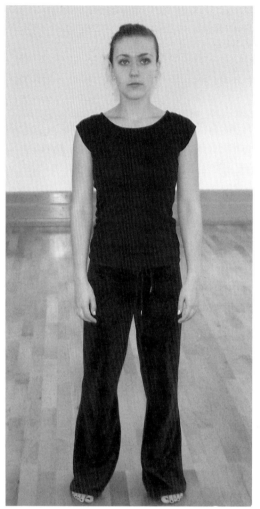 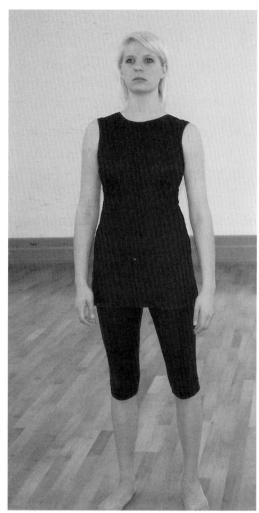

The open body.

your face are light, energized, open and ready for action. Stand in your aligned position with your chest open, your head lifted and your knees loose and relaxed. With this feeling of energy and openness you are now ready to begin to sing.

3   WARMING-UP

In the course of the last chapters you have learned how to release all unnecessary tension from the body and stand in an aligned posture, and you have understood enough of the physiology of the vocal mechanism for effective voice production. However, at the start of any session it is important to carry out some of the release exercises and some of the following warm-up exercises to prepare the body and the mind for singing.

The following exercises are designed so that they can be done by groups led by a musical director, though they can also be done alone. In the second half of this section, therefore, I've assumed that the group will have access to a piano and that the leader will be able to play the starting pitches and read the scored exercises. However, the exercises are also fully explained, so it should be possible to reproduce them with no more than a rudimentary knowledge of music or solfa and a pitch pipe.

If you are practising alone, and working on a particular aspect of your vocal delivery, you can begin the session with these exercises, but you might prefer to replace the first section with the body-release exercises in Chapter 2. You could then use the humming and sirening exercises from this chapter before moving on to Chapters 4 and 5. That way you can focus

The Purpose of the Warm-Up

At the start of each rehearsal of a choir or a musical-theatre company, you should undertake a group warm-up. This serves several purposes: first, and most obviously, it prepares the voice for the muscular exertions required; second, it allows the singer to focus on their own body and release physical tensions and external mental concerns; third, it draws the group into a shared activity ready for the communal rehearsal.

more time and energy on the exercises designed for the part of your voice you have chosen to work on at any particular session.

RELEASING THE BODY

The first task is to release tension and to get the group energized for the session ahead. A really effective way of achieving this is to ask the group to run on the spot or, if you have space, to jog around the room avoiding everyone else. You can elaborate on this by asking the group to change speeds and, if the group are young and fit, by asking them to almost run into someone face to face before pulling out of the way at the last minute. Stress that there is to be no physical contact or you may have accidents. After about half a minute, and at the same time as continuing to jog around or on the spot, ask the group to shake their hands, then their whole arms, then their shoulders, neck and head and finally their whole upper body. They should simultaneously vocalize a 'brr' or 'drr', sliding up and down freely. Sliding up and down is often referred to as 'sirening'.

Continuing to move on the spot, slightly more gently now, massage the face, neck and jaw while vocalizing a loose vowel shape on no particular pitch. Allow the sound to be affected by the movements the massage creates in the face and mouth. The tongue and jaw should hang loosely throughout, and the pitch should be varied so that nothing becomes formal or stiff.

Standing in Alignment

Come to a standing position and check the body's alignment with the ears lined up above the shoulders, over the hips, over the knees (which are gently released rather than tightly straight) and the knees balanced over the arch of the foot.

You are now in a position to carry out the swinging, neck sways and rolling down from Chapter 3 and any of the following release and isolation exercises that you choose. Depending on the needs of your group and the amount of time you have, you may prefer to move straight on to the breathing and humming section below. Alternatively, you can combine the two by including the suggested vocal exercises with each of the physical exercises below; though, especially at first, you will need to get used to the physical and vocal exercises separately.

Shoulder Rolls

Lift the right shoulder at the front and roll it over to drop at the back. Repeat four more times. Repeat the exercise with the left shoulder and then with both together. This releases muscles in the upper thorax and neck.

Additional Vocalization

Breathe in before beginning, then exhale on a 'ssss', sustaining the sound for all five shoulder rolls with the right shoulder, and breathe in again and exhale for all five shoulder rolls with the left shoulder.

Arm Drops

Raise the right arm without lifting the shoulder, then, on a given signal, drop the arm so that it falls (and perhaps slightly swings) at the side. Repeat several times before switching to the other arm.

Body Drops

Stand with both hands raised above the head, but with the shoulders down. In quick succession drop the arms, then the head to the chest, then the torso so that you are hanging from the hips with the knees slightly bent (see page 41). Rebuild by rolling the body up, then raising the head and straightening the arms over the head. Repeat several times so that the effect of dropping is achieved, and speed can be increased, but not until the effect of dropping is comfortably and reliably understood.

Ribs and Hips

These exercises raise awareness of, and strengthen, the torso muscles that will be used to support the work of the diaphragm. They also increase the flexibility and agility of the upper body for breathing and release tensions in the shoulders, back and hips.

Bend your knees slightly and place the hands on the ribs so that the hands act as a reminder to keep the ribs and upper body still. Now swing your hips to the right, then to the left and repeat several times. Now swing the pelvis forward and back several times. Now circle to the right several times, circle to the left several times and finally perform a figure-of-eight with the pelvis.

Optional Vocalization
Breathe in before the exercise, then sustain a gentle hum at a comfortable pitch for as long as is comfortable. Every time you need to breathe in and restart, change the pitch to another part of your voice.

Many people have much more trouble with the following exercise that asks for the same movements from the rib cage. Raise the ribs and place the hands on the hips to act as a reminder to keep the hips still. Move the ribs and upper thorax to the right and to the left. Don't expect a large movement, but try to get a sense of raising the ribs and using the muscles of the waist and upper body. Now carry out the same sequence as above, moving to the front and back, circling both ways and finally moving the ribs in a figure-of-eight pattern.

Optional Vocalization
Carry out the same vocal exercise to accompany the rib movements, but using the sound 'ooh'. Don't worry if the sound wobbles as you move. The important thing is that there is the minimum amount of tension in your face, neck and jaw.

Arm Swinging
Again this exercise is dependent on having sufficient space. It is an energizing, as well as a releasing, exercise. Simply swing the right arm

---

Beginning to Sing

If you haven't carried out the optional vocalizations with the physical exercises above, do them now. They are:
- singing sustained single pitches on a hum and on 'ooh'
- using the consonant 'ng' to slide up and down the full vocal range.

---

in a circle, going up at the front and down at the back, as though doing backstroke with one arm. Wind the speed up and then down again. Repeat with the other arm and then both together.

Optional Vocalization
With the mouth forming the sound 'ng' slide up and down the vocal range, in a rhythmic relationship to the arm swing that is comfortable for you. You could allow the voice to rise for one swing and fall for the second swing and so on, or even allowing two swings to rise and two to fall so that the full range of the voice can be covered.

Finally shake the body, arms and head out again, jogging on the spot while sliding up and down on 'brr' and 'drr'.

WARMING-UP THE VOICE

Falling Octaves
Begin on the A above middle C on an 'ee' sound, then slide down an octave and sustain the finish note, feeling its resonance. Make sure it is a slide (glissando) and remains poised and lifted throughout; there is often a tendency to hop from the top note skirting the middle and landing at the bottom with a thud. Be sure to lift the soft palate (a feeling of start-

ing to yawn) and make space in the mouth for the first note, but avoid contorting the face or mouth. Use 'ee' for the slide and, when you are comfortable with the slide, finish with an 'ah' to feel the vibration and resonance on the final note. Repeat starting a semitone higher each time for about a fifth or about eight times.

Falling octaves.

Rising by Semitones
This exercise moves the voice very gently up the scale, so begin in the lower middle part of the voice, perhaps around middle C. Sing 'oo' on the starting note, rise a semitone on the vowel 'ee' before returning to 'oo' on the first note. Repeat the exercise each time starting a semitone higher.

Rising semitones.

Rising Triplets
The range covered in each exercise is gradually extending, so this time the exercise covers a fifth, but still rising in a scalar fashion. The notes are grouped into threes (triplets), and the first triplet begins on middle C with the sound 'mee'. The whole exercise is sung gently and smoothly (legato). I generally teach this exercise using numbered pitches before introducing the vowel sounds. If you number the notes of the major scale from 1 to 8, the exercise goes: 123 234 345 4321 (DohRayMi RayMiFah MiFahSo FahMiRayDoh). When the group is comfortable with the pattern, switch to different sounds as follows: mee (123), meh (234), mee (345), meh 432, mee (1). This

exercise can then be used to practise the articulation of vowel sounds by removing the consonant 'm' and using different vowels. Once again the whole exercise should be repeated rising over about a fifth.

Rising by step up a third.

The middle part of the voice should now be prepared for two more adventurous and less precise exercises to introduce agility.

Bouncing
I call these bouncing exercises to create the image of the sound leaping lightly from note to note, like a tennis ball that is being tapped repeatedly by the same racket so that it stays aloft. The first exercise involves singing up the first five notes of the scale before bouncing on that fifth note a further five times before rolling back down the scale (DohRayMiFahSo So So So So So SoFahMiRayDoh). I teach this by singing up the scale on 'ah', the arrival on the fifth note counts as 1 and the bounced notes are then sung to 23456. The note is then repeated one more time on 'ah' as the start of the descending scale. Once the pattern is understood, the vowel sound should be varied on each reiteration of the exercise, rising by semitones.

It is important to stress that this exercise should be sung lightly and brightly, just tapping the note rather than giving it any great force or weight. It is useful for agility, but also for feeling the movement of the diaphragm, which provides the bouncing flow of air, and it is also useful to extend the range higher than in previous exercises.

Bouncing the voice lightly.

The second bouncing exercise includes a leap of a fifth and should also be approached lightly and brightly. Using the numbers of the scale practised earlier, this can be taught as follows: 1 5 1 5 54321 (Doh So Doh So SoFahMiRayDoh). The timing is indicated by the spacing. Again it should be practised on all vowels.

Bouncing up a fifth.

Scales to Ninth

It is now time to introduce a larger range and sing scales up to the ninth of the scale on all vowels. There is no rest at the top, but a continuous flowing sound as follows: 1 2 3 4 5 6 7 8 9 8 7 6 5 4 3 2 1

(DohRayMiFahSoLaTiDoRayDoTiLaSoFahMi RayDoh).

Scales to a ninth.

Arpeggios

Next we move on to arpeggios or broken chords, and sing in longer phrases. The broken chord or arpeggio is most commonly made up of the notes 1,3,5 and 8 of the scale in the sequence 1 3 5 8 5 3 1 (Doh Mi Soh Doh Soh Mi Doh). You can build up any sequence on these notes, but the simplest is to run up and down three times using a different vowel sound each time.

Arpeggios.

Leaps

As a final exercise, while working only with vowel sounds it is good to include a large leap. A common exercise is the following one that includes a leap of an octave and then links to the scale to the ninth practised above, but you can extend it to a leap of a tenth and rework the scale down to fit rhythmically and melodically. The basic pattern is: 1 8 _ 78987654321 (Doh, Doh, _ TiDohRayDohTiLaSoFaMiRayDoh) with the beats on the underlined notes.

49

Leaping an octave.

ARTICULATION

To begin the work on articulation, massage the face and carry out some tongue-stretching exercises, as described in Chapter 3 above. Keep vocalizing during these physical exercises, ensuring the release of the tongue, jaw and facial muscles.

To begin to exercise the muscles of the mouth, first run up and down a scale to the fifth using a consonant from each group listed in the table in Chapter 2 above, followed by 'ah' ('pah', 'lah', 'shah', 'kah', etc.). These can be changed at each session by calling out the new sound at the end of each scale.

Now pick a consonant from two different groups and form a simple word (it doesn't have to mean anything), but examples include 'wait' or 'yuck' or 'beat' or 'ship'. Repeat these going up and down the scale, making sure that beginning and ending consonants and the vowel are clear and that the two consonants don't become confused.

Add a second vowel at the end of words to make, for example, 'busy', 'chilly', 'below' or even 'Mona Lisa' and so on. These can be practised up and down scales or arpeggios to allow for constant variation.

Tongue-Twisters
There are very many tongue-twisters that you can practise by setting up a rhythm within the

Common Mistakes

One problem caused by poor articulation is the joining together of the final consonant of one word with the beginning of the next word. This is often a good thing in order to sing smoothly, but can cause the mis-articulation of words, and therefore misunderstanding for the listener. A likely place for this difficulty is before the word 'you', when, for example, 'won't you' becomes 'won choo'. Other examples to practise carefully are those where the final consonant of one word is the same as the first consonant of the next, as in 'up past', 'with thee', 'take care', 'large jar', 'hot tea' or 'some more'. You might also explore the difference between 'A nice house' and 'An ice house', or 'Attend' and 'at end'.

group. I usually begin with 'red leather, yellow leather', which is easier than its counterpart, 'red lorry, yellow lorry'. When it can be repeated at a reasonable pace I like to use it going up and down a scale or arpeggio. 'She sells sea shells on the sea shore' and 'Sister Susie sewing shirts for soldiers' are always fun. You can sing the first line of 'Peter Piper picked a peck of pickled pepper', and then repeat 'Peter Piper picked' so that it fits to the scale to a ninth you have already learnt.

I generally finish this section with some arpeggios that rise for an octave and a half on the tonic chord and fall on the dominant (1351354275421 or DohMiSoDohMiSoFah RayTiSoFahRayDoh) using a repeated word such as 'coffee', or 'chilly'. A favourite phrase among actors is 'equity deputy', and I usually end with 'memeny', not a word at all, but a useful exercise for the lips and tongue.

Arpeggios and articulation.

Before moving on to the work of the session, it is good to sing one or two simple things together. This is helpful for concentration and for getting the group to really listen to each other. The final exercise in this section, therefore, is to sing the theme of the 'William Tell overture' to the words 'many men' repeated. You might want to substitute any other song that the choir knows well and that they enjoy singing.

A song for articulation.

SINGING ROUNDS

Singing rounds is useful for blowing away the cobwebs of concentration, as well as listening to the rest of the group. It is also an effective starting point for harmony singing. Useful rounds are 'Frère Jacques', 'Old Abram Brown', 'London's Burning', 'Rose Rose', which are all scored below. Singing these can also include practice of a range of dynamics and the introduction of subtle variations of volume to allow different voices to be heard. The stars in the examples below mark the points at which different groups enter the round.

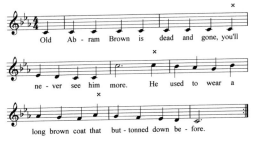

Frère Jacques.

Old Abram Brown.

London's Burning.

Rose, Rose.

Improving Listening

Also for listening within the group, each section of the choir can be given a note of a chord. At signals from the musical director, the choir should increase or decrease the volume, or raise or lower the pitch by a semitone. This takes some working out, but can be really helpful for less-experienced singers, who tend to sharpen when increasing volume or who don't listen carefully to how their voice fits into the chord.

Tuning can be practised by singing up and down the major and minor scales to the days of the week, or singing up and down the months of the year to the chromatic scale. The descending chromatic scale is the most difficult, so the scale should be sung unaccompanied and then the pitch checked at the end.

In order to encourage teamwork, and to balance the volume of all the singers, it is useful to sing a simple nursery rhyme, such as 'Baa baa black sheep', or any other simple song the

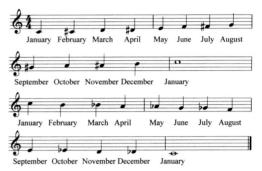

Chromatic months.

group knows well. Then, standing in a circle, each member of the group sings a single word. The rhythm, pitch and dynamic balance of the song must be maintained throughout (though the male voices may be pitched in their own register). As the group becomes more expert, the complexity of the song can be increased.

BEGINNING IMPROVISATION

Improvisation is useful, not only because it frees the individual from inhibitions and allows new sounds to emerge, but because it encourages close and detailed listening and memorizing. If the group wants to develop improvisation skills, the director can begin by encouraging individuals to improvise a short motif or phrase over a single note sustained by the rest of the group. The group are given a single note to sing in unison, breathing when necessary, while each individual in turn is encouraged to introduce a short motif beginning and ending on the sustained note. The motif should move from consonance to dissonance and return rather than simply exploring the notes of the chord. In the early days this might consist of three or five notes, but should develop into longer phrases and patterns.

When the group is comfortable with this, a single chord should be sustained, with the director identifying a note for up to four groups within the choir. This chord should not be a simple major chord, but one that doesn't impose a strong sense of key. It should allow a more ambiguous sense of tonality. It might, for example, be a chord made of fourths, or include discords such as seconds or sevenths. The important thing is that the chord does not enforce a single, harmonic centre. At first, this chord should be used simply as a basis for improvised motifs and patterns to be developed by individuals within the group. Call and response patterns, or question and answer phrases can be developed through improvisation, and possibly longer song structures will gradually be either improvised or composed.

While maintaining the pitch, each section of the choir (singing the same part of the chord) should decide on a rhythm they want to sing on their single note, with the director specifying the time signature – 4/4 is easiest to start with. For example, those on the bass might decide to create a steady pulse of dotted crotchet followed by quaver, repeated. Those above, without the need to articulate the pulse, can create syncopated or complex rhythms that work with the pulse, perhaps introducing triplets or cross rhythms as the group becomes more comfortable with this work. Alternatively the whole group can clap or tap the pulse to maintain a rhythmic centre. When the basic pattern is established, simple motifs and phrases can be improvised above it.

A further development is that the group can alternate two chords in a shifting, rhythmic pattern that provides a rhythmic texture over which more extensive improvisations can be developed. Gradually more and more complex textures can be established above which melodic improvisation can be explored.

Now the group is warmed up physically and vocally, and has begun to work together and concentrate, it is time to move on to working on a particular song. However, before I look at songs for individuals in the later chapters of the book, in the next two chapters I will introduce some more exercises for individuals working alone to develop their own voices.

4 DEVELOPING THE VOICE 1

The exercises in the next two chapters are designed to provide an incremental development, building up technical proficiency. Each of the six sections spread over the two chapters: Breathing Exercises, From Speaking to Singing, Improving Tone and Dynamic Range, Changing Volume, Flexibility, Using Vibrato and Colouring the Voice, is also arranged incrementally. Although your focus in any particular session may be on one of these areas, you would be well-advised to incorporate some material from each of these sections in this order in every practice. So, for example, a beginner might spend a whole session working through the breathing exercises and just touching on the speaking to singing section. When a little more advanced the same singer might use some of the release and warm-up exercises above, then one or two of their favourite breathing exercises and a couple of speaking to singing exercises before spending the majority of the session on flexibility. At an even more advanced stage, the singer might choose to use some of these exercises and substitute others with exercises they have learned elsewhere that have the same purpose as these, before focusing on the vibrato or vocal colouring sections of this guide. The important thing to remember,

though, is that these exercises are arranged incrementally in terms of learning, but also incrementally in terms of technical difficulty and vocal preparation. This is because it is important that at every practice the singer should work through a process before attempting, for example, the vocal colouring exercises, so that the voice is adequately prepared for what are more demanding exercises. So, always begin with something from each section, but you don't necessarily need to do everything from each section before moving on.

BREATHING EXERCISES

The first exercises are intended to help you locate the muscles and bones that will help you sustain and extend your breath.

First, put one hand on your ribs with your thumb pointing to your back and your fingers spread out around the front of your ribs. You should feel two or three ribs with your fingers, though your little finger may rest on the flesh above and around your waist. Place your other hand just above your waist on the front of your body. You should feel the edges of your ribs and the gap between them. Now yawn and feel the expansion in your ribs as they lift sideways and can direct into a controlled sound. At the same time, you must always be conscious that the placing of the hands and the feeling of expansion does not lead to tension in the shoulders. When you are entirely secure in breathing fully in this way you may choose to use one hand or the other, or neither, but placing the hands is often an effective way to focus the mind on a part of the body at the start of a session.

Now breathe in again, and this time, hum very gently at a comfortable pitch on the out breath. Try to sustain the sound, by resisting the urge to let the ribs drop immediately. Instead, concentrate on contracting them slowly. Don't worry if the sound wobbles. If you sustain the sound for as long as you are able and then a little longer, without creating tension in your throat or shoulders, you will discover that when you stop your body will automatically inhale quickly and fully. This is the most efficient form of in-breath, as a chemical reaction in the body responds to the shortage of oxygen and instructs the muscles to take in air.

Now move your central hand down below your waist to feel your abdomen. Go back over these exercises and focus on allowing the abdomen to release on each inhalation. You might feel that your body is becoming a barrel filled with air that is slowly released. Notice the difference in the amount of air and the depth of the breath when you consciously release your diaphragm and let your stomach release outwards. When you inhale, keep the ribs lifted and allow the diaphragm to push the air out first. Only allow the ribs to contract in a controlled way afterwards.

Quicker Inhalation and Exhalation

You now have the basic mechanics for breathing in songs with a sustained line and plenty of

Feeling rib and diaphragm movements.

back and the diaphragm expands to draw air into the body. Feel the release at the end of the yawn as the air is expelled.

This time, without yawning, breathe in through the nose or the mouth and feel the same amount of expansion of the ribs and diaphragm. Notice that these breaths are very deep and that they require a lot of energy, but that they produce a lot of breath, which you

time to breathe, but that is not always sufficient. Sometimes you need to breathe in more
quickly, and sometimes you need to take less
air and blow it out with more attack.

A sniff or gasp of surprise gives you the sensation of breathing in quickly, or taking in a
snatch breath that doesn't cause tension in the
shoulders. Try each of these with one hand on
your diaphragm. Feel the strength of the
diaphragm first when you sniff, and then as
you gasp in surprise. The difference between
these two is clearly that sniffing is done
through the nose, and gasping takes air
through the mouth. So practise these to get
used to the short, sharp intake of breath with
the incorporation of the diaphragm. But, of
course, when singing, you need to be able to
accomplish these silently, so the next step is to
practice the mechanics of these inhalations as
soundlessly as possible.

Next you need to feel the effects of a
stronger exhalation, and to do this you should
practise blowing out candles, both real and
imaginary. With your hand on your abdomen
again, blow out ten candles on a birthday
cake, one at a time. Don't pay any attention to
the in-breath, just concentrate on the repeated
attack of blowing out each of ten candles. Feel
how the diaphragm pushes out sufficient air
for the job and then recoils to take in enough
air for the next candle.

Now try counting to ten on a comfortable
singing pitch, all on the same note, and with
exactly the same attack as you used to blow
out the candles. Notice how much bigger,
more directed, and more resonant your sound
has become already.

This time, you need to blow out all ten candles in one exhalation, or you might imagine
the air as a fountain on which you balance a
ball. Put your hand an inch or two in front of

your mouth and allow it to be blown away
until you can't feel the breath on your hand
any more. Now try the same thing on the
vowel 'oo'. The breath is released much less
quickly, and the sound produced is strong and
focused.

You will now be starting to feel the energy
that is created by the breath, but also the effort
that is required in the muscles of the thorax
and abdomen to inhale and exhale strongly,
and so direct and support the voice. Make sure
you are conscious that you are not tightening
your throat at any point in these exercises.

Once you have become accustomed to taking breath in by expanding the ribs and
releasing the diaphragm at various speeds,
and blowing air out either with a sustained or
attacking exhalation, try the following exercises. You can gradually increase the length of
time taken to sing the exhalation, but never
continue if tension begins to creep into the
shoulders, throat or jaw.

Exercises for Regular Practice in Groups
Breathe in slowly over a count of four then
hum on the exhalation for a count of twelve.
Each exhalation will be sustained for two extra
counts. The start and end points of this exercise can be altered, as can the pace of the
counting. There are further variations on this
exercise that you can practise to ring the
changes. These involve singing a note higher
on each exhalation, or introducing different
vowel sounds to replace the hum, or hissing
instead of humming. However, you should
read the section on warming up before introducing these variations.

The following exercise encourages a speed-
ier inhalation as the time allowed for
inhalation is gradually reduced, and the
length of the exhalation increases. Again try

this on a hum until you are completely comfortable before experimenting with any variations you care to introduce.

Breathe in for four counts (in 4).
Hum out for twelve counts (out 12).
Breathe in for three counts (in 3).
Hum out for fourteen counts (out 14).
Breathe in for two counts (in 2).
Hum out for sixteen counts (out 16).
Breathe in for one count (in 1).
Hum out for eighteen counts (out 18).
Breathe in for one count (in 1).
Hum out for twenty counts (out 20).

Changing Positions

The final stage is to be able to continue breathing, and therefore singing, in a relaxed manner no matter what position you are in. One of the features of musical-theatre performance is that it requires you to sing in places that are appropriate for the character and situation but may not be ideal for singing. In order to get used to maintaining control of the support mechanism and releasing tension from the jaw, throat and shoulders when singing, you should explore breathing and humming exercises in a range of unconventional positions. Begin by practising these breathing exercises while sitting and lying down. You might also try them during and after jogging to simulate the effect of singing and dancing together. Joan Melton, in her book *One Voice* encourages her students to vocalize while in various yoga positions. This may or may not suit you, but it is interesting and useful to explore vocalizing while undertaking exercise, and linking physical warm-up exercises to vocal ones; so try these exercises whatever activity you are doing, whether exercise or housework, in the bath and in the garden. This way you will allow a pattern of energetic breathing and the production of controlled sustained or attacking sounds to become a part of your everyday life, rather than a separate activity that you set aside time to practise formally at certain times and places.

FROM SPEAKING TO SINGING

The voice is the same instrument whether speaking or singing, though it is used in a more sustained and supported manner in singing, and with a greater sense of openness in the mouth and throat. This is really important in musical theatre because there are often occasions (which will be discussed in more detail later) in which the introduction for a song incorporates a development from spoken to sung text. The following exercises are therefore targeted at maintaining a consistent vocal quality when moving from speaking to singing.

You have already become used to falling patterns. This time begin with a sigh that has a breathy quality. Now, using the same pitch range, sigh again, but this time with a more focused (less breathy) sound and using a clean vowel. Practise this on a range of pitches and both rising and falling, and on all the vowels. The third stage is to sustain the first and last notes, but to slide between them. Finally, experiment with a combination of scales and slides, so you might begin with a scale up five notes, slide back down and up again before singing the scale down to finish. Using a combination of scales and slides will allow you to introduce new exercises to maintain innovation and interest, and to extend the vocal range as you are ready and able. But bear in mind that when you yawn and vocalize the sound, you will discover that your vocal range is much larger than you think, and these exercises will allow you to begin to incorporate that larger range into your singing voice. Most important, however, is that whenever you explore the wider range of your voice, make sure that you keep returning to the release exercises and don't allow facial contortions or bodily tension, especially in the throat and jaw, to interfere. Go slowly and keep checking your body.

The next stage is to introduce a whole range of short phrases and add melodies to them. You can begin by saying the phrase on one note; for example, 'make a cup of tea' spoken on a single pitch. The beauty of this phrase is that it starts with the hum (m) and ends with an open and resonant vowel (ee). Now sing the phrase on one note. The first thing to be aware of is that the voice feels more focused onto the tongue and upper palate if you articulate the phrase clearly, whether in speaking or singing. Secondly, think about the 'm' at the beginning of the phrase and how the hum vibrates the lips. The lips then open for the 'eh' and 'ee' sounds before the back of the tongue forms the 'k'. Think through the rest of the phrase analysing the articulation before focusing on the final vowel 'ee' and ensuring that it is as resonant as possible. Now improvise a series of melodic phrases to these words using scales and small intervals or repeated pitches.

You can use any verbal patterns to develop singing exercises, but I like to work with everyday phrases rather than poetry, so that the importance of communication is constantly reinforced. Next you might ask 'do you want milk in your coffee?'. This is a good phrase to sing, except that the natural inclination is to ask the question by jumping up on the word 'milk' and then running down the scale (as in the score). In order to achieve a good sound on the higher note and the word 'milk' you need to be sure to sing a clear 'I' sound rather than swallowing the vowel and only vocalizing the consonants. This is an example of where singing requires a slightly altered articulation of the words, so that the resonance of vowels is extended and the percussive effect of consonants shortened. Practise singing the word 'milk' on its own by singing a long 'miii-iii' before, right at the end, adding a short but clear 'lk'. Now go back to singing the whole phrase and remember to sing the final word fully, don't drop the end of the word 'coffee', but make the final vowel clear and resonant.

Do you want milk in your coffee?

Make a cup of tea.

You can find musical patterns for the following phrases or make up your own:

- Do the washing-up.
- Clear the table.
- Stand and deliver.

Suggested melodies for these phrases are included below.

First of all, explore the vowels and consonants to find the maximum resonance for the phrase. Then explore the way that different melodies suggest a different expression or meaning in the words. For example, if the emphasis is on '<u>Do</u> the washing-up', an order or instruction is suggested, whereas, 'Do the <u>washing</u>-up' might be interpreted as having a sense of frustration at the repetitive task.

Do the washing-up.

The alteration of the pitch shape alters the sense too, as in the high-pitched instruction '<u>Stand</u> and deliver' in the final example. So you can make up phrases of your own to explore in which you attempt to achieve the maximum resonance from the vowels but clear articulation of the consonants and a sense of emotional meaning in the overall rhythm and shape of the phrase.

IMPROVING TONE AND DYNAMIC RANGE

In the section above, I identified the need for the voice to maintain consistent sound from speech to song. Likewise, although the voice changes to some extent as it changes pitch, there should be no gear changes or sudden alterations as the voice moves across its more difficult patches. In addition, you will need to develop the ability to change volume without altering the tone colour. At the end of this you will have control of the tone colour so that if you choose to make a breathy sound you will be able to. However, if you need to (or choose to) maintain a focused sound across pitch ranges and dynamic changes, you will also be able to do that.

A focused or resonant sound is that sound created when the air passes through the vocal folds with the appropriate amount of resistance, rises through the released musculature of the throat and is focused onto the hard palate to create vibrations that resonate through the bony structures of the head and face. You will be able to feel the sounds vibrate if you place your hands on your neck, chest and face when they are sung at the optimum pitches. Certain pitches and vowel sounds cause greater vibrations in certain parts of the body. The sound created has a ring or buzz that you need to learn to identify. For example, sing an 'ee' sound on a low or mid-range note with your hands placed over your cheeks and neck. Feel the vibration of that tone and listen to the sound of your voice (remembering that the sound others hear is different to the sound you hear). Mark that sound for yourself as a resonant tone.

Now try an 'ah' sound at a lower pitch with your hands on your neck and chest. If you let the note sink down it will not be resonant but will sound dark and heavy. However, if you slightly raise your cheek bones as though about to smile, the breath can be focused onto the hard palate and the vibrations will increase. Again, you need to find the resonant sound and mark it for yourself.

The task now is to maintain that resonance while varying the pitch and volume of the note. There are three sets of exercises for doing this: the first varies the vowel sound on the same note; the second varies the note on the same vowel sound; and the third varies the volume at first on the same pitch, but gradually in association with all the other variations.

Practise Little and Often

You should work a little on each of the following sets of exercises each time you practise, rather than attempting to make a dramatic change to one part of the voice at a time. Remember, you are developing muscles and becoming used to new forms of activity and use. As with all muscles, they respond to regular practice, but they can be damaged or become easily tired (so that damage occurs) by sudden dramatic changes in the type and amount of activity.

Changing Vowels

On a single note, sing a series of vowels. Begin with the vowel that is most resonant for you; so, for example, on a low or mid-range pitch, I might start with 'ee', and then sing 'eh'. Alternate between these two vowels, making sure that the shape of the mouth and tongue is clear and that the movement of the tongue between the two vowels is accomplished cleanly with energy. Now move up a semitone

and repeat the exercise. Do this up and down a comfortable range in your voice.

Changing vowels.

When you are used to this pattern pick two other vowels to work with (perhaps 'oo' and 'aw', or 'ah' and 'eh') and then extend the exercise to three vowels (ah, eh, ee, eh, ah) and finally to five (ah, eh, ee, aw, oo). Once you are used to the clear articulation of the vowels you will also be able to increase the speed of change, but begin slowly so that you have time to check the resonance, the vowel shape and the precision of movement between vowels.

Changing Pitch

In the warm-up section, I introduced a range of scales and arpeggios that you can use here but, as with the exercises above, begin very slowly so that you can hear the clarity of the vowel shape and the resonance of the sound on each pitch. Begin with a simple five-note scale practised on each vowel sound in turn. Begin with the sound that is most resonant for you, probably 'ee' or 'oo'. Very slowly sing up and down the scale. If you find any problems, or places where the voice seems to break or wobble, check for tension and release it. You should also go back and repeat some earlier exercises: slide down over that part of the voice, then sing down over that part, then sing back up again while trying to maintain the same placing, release and resonance.

Gradually you will want to extend the range, so incorporate the scales to an octave and a ninth and all the different arpeggio pat-

Increasing Volume

To increase volume you need to increase the air pressure by sending more air from the lungs. You do this by increasing the support from the diaphragm. This increases the pressure of air at the vocal cords creating a bigger sound. Make sure that all the other muscles are as released as usual, and that the sound is directed to the resonators. Do not push! You may need to make sure that you are opening your mouth enough to allow the sound out, but avoid opening your mouth wider as the means of increasing sound. This will lead to pushing with muscles in the neck and throat, create an unpleasant sound, and could cause problems in the future.

terns from earlier chapters, so that you can sing up and down your whole vocal range without any alteration in the tone of the voice.

CHANGING VOLUME

To get used to the idea of speaking and singing loudly, begin by directing words or instructions to someone else. If you can't think of anything else, simply say 'hey' or count to five. Gradually increase the distance between you and, at the same time, make sure you are still being heard, but do not shout. Now examine the difference in how you speak at that volume. You are likely to find that your speech has slowed down, you will certainly be articulating much more clearly, you may have raised the pitch of your speech, you will probably be opening your mouth wider, and you will certainly be using more breath. Plainly, you cannot sing more slowly every time you need to increase volume, and you are now

discovering how clearly you should have been articulating all the time, but the energy, and the focus and resonance of the voice required, now becomes apparent.

Now try the same exercise but singing the words and sustaining the sound. You are trying to achieve a very resonant sound that fills the space and causes vibrations all around you. You should have the feeling of expanding your sound so that it resounds off the walls of a good sized room – and don't use the bathroom, that's cheating.

When you have got over the shock of creating a larger sound, begin to incorporate that new range into some singing exercises. Begin with a sustained note on your most resonant vowel. Start quietly and increase and then decrease the volume. There is often a tendency for the pitch of the note to be affected, so concentrate on maintaining the pitch. Secondly, when you decrease the volume don't let the sound become less resonant. It is easy for the sound to become poorly produced rather than a resonant quiet sound. To avoid this you will need to maintain the flow of breath support

Enjoying Your Voice

Many people constrict their voices by speaking on the breath, swallowing words or not articulating clearly, not opening their mouths or covering their mouths with their hands, or dropping chin, shoulders and neck, so that the voice isn't focused or directed out. One of the first things many people struggle with, when beginning to sing, is that you need to enjoy making a sound, and directing it out so that it fills the space with your vibrant presence.

from the diaphragm. Practise this exercise on all vowels and at all pitches.

Changing volume.

When you have got control of the increase and decrease of volume, once on a single note, start increasing the pace of dynamic change so that you get louder and softer several times in the course of one long note. Finally, introduce a small movement of pitch, trilling slowly from one note to the one above. At the same time alter the volume, but not so that one note is louder than the other. You might use a pattern of threes so that three notes are loud followed by three quieter and so on. Gradually build up the pace at which you can do this.

Changing volume and pitch.

Now you can start changing pitch at the same time as altering volume. Listen very carefully to your sound while doing these exercises, though. Increasing volume as you raise the pitch can easily become pushed or forced, and can sound very ugly, especially if you have accomplished it by increasing tension in the neck or jaw rather than by increasing the breath pressure.

Begin by sliding up and down a fifth as you have done before, using a clean vowel sound. Practise increasing the volume as you rise and decreasing the volume as you fall, then reverse the pattern so that you decrease as you rise and increase as you fall. Both of these need control, but the second is usually harder. Try this on a range of pitches and on all vowel sounds.

Next do the same exercises but using scales. This time the important thing is to make sure that each note is a very small amount louder or quieter, so that the increase or decrease is gradual and there is not a sudden change in the volume.

When you are comfortable with all these stages, you can start putting different parts of the exercises together to test your mental and physical agility. For example, you could run up and down a scale, changing the vowel every two or three notes and at the same time introduce volume changes as you rise or fall, or even, for each set of two or three notes. However, it is really important that you don't try these tricky mental tests until you have formed excellent habits in each of the exercises slowly and separately, or it will all fall apart. It is easy to move onto more difficult exercises and not have time to check that there is no undue tension, that the sound is resonant throughout the exercise, or that the vowel sounds are clearly articulated. When you can maintain all these at the same time you are well on your way to introducing words and singing songs.

5 DEVELOPING YOUR VOICE 2

This chapter contains more advanced exercises for developing your voice so that you are able to sing in a range of styles effectively. The exercises should be developed incrementally in each section, as instructed at the start of Chapter 4.

FLEXIBILITY

Like all muscles the vocal cords need regular exercise to improve their flexibility and agility. So far the exercises have been predominantly slow and careful, allowing time to think, listen and feel so that unnecessary tension is not allowed to creep into the vocal delivery. However, speed, flexibility and agility are also important tools for the singer of musical theatre, they allow the singer to articulate highly ornamented melodies, leaps, turns and scales. Once you are confident of your ability to accomplish all the exercises so far without introducing tension or reproducing the habits of particular musical styles, you should start to increase the agility of your voice and therefore your ability to sing at a greater pace.

Listen to any R'n'B singer and note the ornamentation of the melody line, but also listen to the tension that is used in the creation of the sound. Listen to the stylistic twitch at the end of the phrase as the tension and support

are audibly released. There is a similar feature, a dropping off at the end of each phrase, in rock music, and most pop music uses a glottal stop at the start of many words beginning with vowels. You need to be able to reproduce these sounds, but you also need to be able to sing without these stylistic idiosyncrasies, so that you can sing in many styles and with as little tension as possible.

Trills

Begin by playing with any note that is comfortable in your range and its neighbour using a smooth phrasing (creating a legato sound) on a single vowel. First try alternating with the next note above, and then explore the next note below. The natural inclination will be to rise a whole tone. Do this, but also find the semitone and see how easy it is to rise and fall rapidly between the two notes. Begin with two pitches arranged into a rhythmic group of five (note, note above, note, note above, note), then proceed to seven and nine notes in your phrase, but still with only two pitches. Practise this exercise on all vowel sounds until you feel comfortable.

When you are certain that the tuning of these notes is secure, change the rhythmic pattern so that you are singing groups of three notes (triplets). This means that the accent will alternate as follows: A B A, B A B, A B A, B A B, A. The last single note is sustained to create a sense of finality. This phrase is written out on page 62 in the previous chapter. With this exercise you can also ring the changes by beginning with a rising or falling movement of a tone or semitone (inverting the phrase), and you can gradually extend the length and increase the pace. Some more variations that you can play with are included in the examples below.

Beginning trills.

More trills.

The following examples are different versions of these exercises that contain trills and turns extending over a greater range. All of the examples should be practised in a comfortable pitch range, gradually extending outwards and on all vowels. At first work at a pace at which you can continue the phrase in a regular pattern. The important thing is that the articulation of the notes is regular and smooth, not lumpy and periodic, as it is likely to be when you begin. Only when you can

articulate these patterns smoothly should you increase the pace.

Trills and turns.

Turns rising.

Next you can extend the range of notes within the exercises ever further by singing the five-, eight- and nine-note scales as practised above, but this time introducing rhythmic variations by using triplet patterns, repeated notes or descending a step at regular intervals. Some examples are given below, but once you have mastered these you should continue to make up new variations for yourself. With all these exercises you should sometimes sing accompanied by the notes on a piano (if possible), so that you are certain of the patterns; but on other occasions you should sing

Increasing agility.

unaccompanied, so that you can make sure that your intonation (tuning) is what you intend. At all times observe the resonance of the sound and the feeling in the muscles of the throat, face and jaw and release any tension that creeps in.

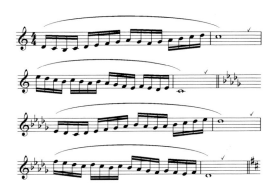

Extending scales.

Staccato (Short, Crisp Notes)

The glottal stop is a feature of pop singing, and it is a useful device for emphasizing words that begin with a vowel. However, it is imperative that you can begin phrases and sing staccato (short and crisp) vowels without a glottal stop, instead using the diaphragm to activate the breath and begin the sound. The overuse of the glottal attack can cause damage to the vocal cords because it relies on increasing the pressure and tension at the cords in order to preface the release of sound. It is useful, though, and so a feature that you should practise, but since most people create the glottal attack as a means of emphasis in everyday speech, the important thing here is to learn to create short, attacking sounds without its explosive tension.

In order to sing a note without a glottal attack, take a breath in, raise the soft palate by feeling as though you are about to yawn and prepare to sing a confident and vibrant 'aah' but with a smooth start to the sound. In order to do this, the vocal cords need to be open and prepared before the breath is propelled through the cords. Practise all the vowel sounds with this amount of preparation. Now try the much harder attack of the glottal stop. Feel the pulling back of the tongue and the closure of the cords. The breath builds up behind the closed cords so that when they open there is an explosive attack. Practice this with all the vowel sounds too, but be aware of releasing the tension immediately after the attack or you could develop a habit of singing with tension in the throat and cords.

Say the words 'eat your dinner' in a calm voice and listen to the opening articulation of the 'e' sound. Another phrase you might practice is 'any dream will do'. Feel and listen to whether the breath begins the phrase in a relaxed way or whether there is a hard edge at the start of the initial vowel. Without the glottal attack there is an openness in the throat at the start of the phrase. Now, pretend you're angry or frustrated by a child who will not eat and so you articulate much more strongly, accenting the beginning of the word 'eat'. Listen to the percussive explosion of the vocal cords that creates a hard edge at the start of the word. Try the same explosion on the second phrase or any other word beginning with a vowel. This is a glottal stop or glottal attack. Identify the difference between those two sorts of attack and practise both methods of beginning the phrase until you are confident of the difference. Now sing those two phrases on any notes both with and without the glottal attack and notice that without the attack you need to maintain the openness of the throat at the start of the phrase.

Now that you are aware of the difference

Glottal Attack or Onset

If you listen to pop singers you will discover that they use a glottal attack very frequently, and many people who have learned to sing by listening to pop music will find it hard to rid themselves of this habit, especially when singing in that style. It is important to persevere, however, so that you can articulate a range of emotions and sing in a range of styles. In addition, because of the explosive pressure on the cords that the glottal stop requires, and the potential for not fully releasing the tension in the throat, overuse of glottal attacks can cause long-term damage to the voice.

between articulating a vowel with and without a glottal stop, you can practise staccato singing, which needs to be accomplished without a glottal attack. First remind yourself of the 'blowing the candles out' exercise above and feel the diaphragm shooting a series of small blasts of air through the lips. The same use of the diaphragm is required in staccato singing, but now the breath is used to make short sounds, like little darts, that resonate on the hard palate. Another way to get a sense of this type of sound is to laugh while placing one hand on the diaphragm. The diaphragm need not make large movements, but it is essential to get a sense that the articulation is generated from the breath and not from the explosive closure of the vocal cords.

The following exercises are for staccato singing, but you can also make up your own exercises or continue to work on the bouncing exercises on page 49. The beginning staccato example remains within quite a limited vocal

range, but once you have mastered these localized areas of vocal agility it is time to extend the range of pitches in some exercises for even greater agility. The staccato and descending intervals is an example of an exercise that introduces larger leaps within a simple staccato pattern that can be inverted or reversed.

Beginning staccato.

Staccato and descending intervals.

Leaps and Ornamentation

The third phase of increasing the flexibility of your voice is to introduce leaps, as well as ornamentation, so that the flexibility and control of intonation and rhythm are not localized. The simplest way to create your own exercises to develop agility is to add ornamentation to exercises you are already practising. So, for example, you can add an ornament, such as a turn, to each step of an arpeggio as in the example below.

Turns and arpeggios falling.

Turns and arpeggios rising and falling.

Finally, the most difficult intervals of all are the chromatic ones. Two exercises are written out below that require first a combination of semitones and leaps, and in the second, an unexpected combination of semitones, tones and leaps. These are designed to be awkward, but once learnt, require you to become accustomed to light, running patterns with unexpected intonation. This sort of exercise is particularly useful in preparing you for the slight alterations in pattern that are a feature of the work of Stephen Sondheim. Think, for example, of the intricacy of the melody Cinderella sings in 'On the steps of the palace' in *Into the Woods* or, for men, Tobias' introduction to 'Pirelli's miracle elixir' in *Sweeney Todd*.

Intonation exercise 1.

Intonation exercise 2.

USING VIBRATO AND COLOURING THE VOICE

In the same way that it is important in musical theatre to be able to sing in a range of styles, it is important to be able to colour the voice in ways appropriate to the character. Colouring the voice includes the use of vibrato, but it also includes developing an understanding of the tonal range available to the singer through the introduction of colour. We will consider vibrato first.

Vibrato

Vibrato is the creation of a pulse or wave in the sound of the voice by the fluctuation of air as it passes over the vocal cords. This causes a variation in volume and the creation of a very small variation in pitch. Wind players produce vibrato in a similar way, by creating a fluctuation in the air that passes into the body of the instrument, though you will notice that they often also vibrate their finger on a key to cause a slight variation in pitch. For string players, vibrato is created by rolling the finger on the string rapidly backwards and forwards. This creates a variation in pitch rather than in volume. However it is created, vibrato can be added to a note to make a more finished or polished sound, while notes without vibrato sound simpler and more direct. Think of the difference in sound produced by a young choirboy without vibrato and that of an opera singer with a very polished and controlled use of vibrato.

The important thing about using vibrato, as with the glottal stop, is that you need to be able to use it at will. As suggested above, vibrato suggests a sense of polish, finish or refinement, which might be perfect for the character you are playing. However, if you are supposed to be representing a naïve or young character, or someone speaking directly and truthfully, you might want to reduce the amount of vibrato used, so that the voice represents that aspect of the character.

Vibrato can be created in the throat by fluttering the vocal cords (which is not recommended). If you imitate the 'baa' of a sheep or the rattle of a machine gun, this is what you are doing. It produces a sound that is used in some singing styles, such as in some types of Middle-Eastern singing. However, there is a similar type of throat vibrato produced by a movement of the larynx that is used in some sorts of pop singing, especially among torch singers, and in jazz and blues singing. If you watch carefully, you will see movement in the throat and tongue, and even sometimes in the jaw, as the whole larynx moves up and down. It tends to produce a vibrato that is slower and wider in pitch and therefore more likely to lead to singing out of tune. This is because the tension it produces can flatten pitch. There is also the possibility that the wide vibrato leads to a seeming inability to control the voice, which then in a circular route leads to tightness in the jaw and tongue in order to control the voice. For all these reasons it is not ideal, though it can be effective at moments of high-emotional drama. Even at these moments, it is perhaps best mixed with the safer vibrato produced from the diaphragm.

To produce vibrato from the diaphragm you need to maintain the support of the abdominal muscles and the open, released muscles of the throat and mouth, while introducing a pulse into the airflow. Sustain a tone in a comfortable vocal range on the sound 'ee'. By the pressure of the abdomen introduce a fluctuation in the constant flow of air that is much smaller than that used for staccato singing. If you place your hand on the diaphragm you should not feel the kick of the pulse but the smooth constant pressure of the airflow. Practise this a little and often with the intention of creating a regular rhythmic pulse rather than a spasmodic and lumpy interruption of the sound. Begin with a smooth sound and then try to produce three pulses before the end of the note, then five and so on.

When you are comfortable with that process, try singing a slow five-note scale and, on each note, sing first in a smooth tone and then introduce a small amount of vibrato. On each note introduce the same length of vibrato. At the end of each note you should finish the sound gently. There can be a tendency to increase the tension in the sound, which is then released in an audible exhalation at the end of the note. If you notice this, go back to an earlier stage and check that you are not using too much tension in the throat or pressure from the abdomen. Try not to let the pitch wobble.

Finally, sing a vocal phrase, perhaps the phrase 'any dream will do', using the notes written by Andrew Lloyd Webber in the musical *Joseph*, or make up your own tune. The important thing is that you sing a series of words and sustain the final open vowel sound and introduce vibrato to create a polished tone that gives a sense of completion to the phrase. Alternatively, pick a song you know well, but at this stage it needs to be a slow song and the phrase you pick needs to finish with an open vowel. Equally important, do not pick a song from a very ornamented pop tradition, such as soul, especially in a version that you know well from a particular singer's performance. That might lead you to try to introduce a combination of ornament and vibrato at the same time. At this point you would be better advised to pick songs that you know from general cultural knowledge, such as folk songs or popular classics (of the 30s–70s) that you have heard sung in many ways by many singers. One of my favourites is 'I can't help falling in love with you', which fulfils all the requirements for practising vibrato.

Colouring the Voice

In addition to vibrato there are a range of vocal colours that you can use to alter the sound of your voice. You will find that when we move onto thinking about the interpretation of songs in the following chapters, the colour of your sound will to some extent alter,

---

Vocal Colour

Many people speak of the head voice, the chest voice, the nasal voice, the mask of the face and so on. In fact the resonance of the voice is produced, as described above, by the impact of vibrations on the hard palate, but the sound can be coloured by increasing or decreasing the amount of vibration that passes from there into different parts of the body. There is the sensation that the sound resonates in these different parts of the body, or even that the sound is produced in the various cavities of the body, when in fact it is the effect of vibration passing into the cavities. However, the range of vocal colours available is increased by understanding how to incorporate these vibrations.

---

in what seems an automatic or natural way, in response to your understanding of the meaning of words and character. However, it is useful to identify the possibilities that are available and discover how to use them before moving on to singing complete songs.

There are many different names for these vocal colours, but most voice books talk about head resonance, the mask of the face and nasal resonance, and the chest voice. In most cases, the books suggest that these areas of resonance can be used alone or can be mixed to produce a wide palette of vocal colours. Gillyanne Kayes' book *Singing and the Actor*, which advocates the Jo Estill method, is rather more technical than many others and uses six names for various vocal colours. These are: speech, falsetto, twang, opera quality, belt and cry. Kayes explains that, in general, most singers are already producing most of these sounds by listening and reproducing vocal qualities, but that developing a thorough understanding of the mechanics of the vocal qualities would require attendance at workshops. However, you can explore the various colours or qualities that are available in your voice. You will then have the opportunity to attempt various colour mixtures in the second half of the book when addressing the interpretation of particular songs.

There is also a misconception that these vocal colours relate to the pitch of the note. In fact that is not true, as a head colour can be used quite low in the register. It generally has a light and controlled quality. A chest resonance, on the other hand, can be mixed with the resonance from the mask of the face to produce a belt sound to above the middle range of the voice. It is a colour that can be used to add breadth and passion to the sound.

The head voice is produced by having the

sensation of yawning and lifting the eyes as though about to smile. The tone colour is light and the sound controlled. To find the sensation of using the head resonance, begin with a pitch that is middle- to high-range in your voice, and sing down the scale while retaining the sense of placement you began with. Many singers have the sensation that there is a vibration in their head and around their eyes when using this colour.

The mask of the face and the nasal resonance is useful for projecting sound. It cuts through but is not attractive in its own right. You were introduced to the nasal resonance in Chapter 1, which is unlikely to be used on its own unless for a particular character. However, it is useful to get a sense of a forward placement on the mask of the face for the articulation of wordy songs. Prefacing any vowel with an n or m will introduce mask resonance, but listen to the difference between these two consonants. N will tend to introduce the reedier sound from the nasal cavities, while m will stimulate vibration in the mouth, lips and around the eyes. In both cases, however, if you place your fingers gently on the sides of your nose or over your mouth you will feel the vibration being produced. Use each of these in turn to preface a simple five-note scale, maintaining the hand position on the face so that you can feel the vibration, and listen to the different qualities you can produce. This type of sound quality will be present in almost everything you sing as it aids articulation and projection, but is particularly useful for fast, wordy songs or for articulating comedy lyrics.

The chest colour adds roundness and mellowness to the tone and can be used to add depth of emotion or passion. This is a very open sound, and to create it you need to have the sensation of yawning again so that you have an open throat, but also of your entire torso becoming an open barrel. Keep your tongue forward, then, without pushing down with the jaw or letting the tongue slip back, in the lower part of your register sing a loud and angry word. 'No' is a good one to start with. Now try the word 'cry' as in 'cry me a river'. Make sure that you sing on the first half of the diphthong – the 'ah' sound. Remember that the sound still needs to vibrate against the hard palate of the mouth, so don't make the sound too dark or swallowed or it will have no carrying power.

Having discovered all these colours, play with them throughout your entire range. Each colour, although it appears to have a convenient pitch range, can be used throughout your range. Before finishing this chapter you need to be confident of using all these colours and mixing them throughout your vocal range. Even when you are ready to move on to singing whole songs in the next chapter, you should maintain regular practice to continue to develop your vocal skills.

PART 2

DEVELOPING THE SONG

6 DEVELOPMENT OF THE MUSICAL

Before going on to explore how you can put all the technical expertise you have now developed into practice in some songs, I'm going to provide a little contextual information about musical theatre. There are two reasons for this. First, I include examples of songs from a number of shows below that you might want to look at to find songs for your repertoire. These include songs for heroes and heroines, comedy songs, patter songs, character songs, and rock and pop songs, some of which are included in the discussions in the following chapters. Second, when you find a song that suits your voice and start developing an approach to it, you need to understand the context for the song. That includes not only the situation in the musical that inspires the character to sing, but also the style of singing and vocal quality that might be appropriate for an interpretation by that character in a particular type of musical set in, or written in, a particular time period. In order to make these decisions it's important to have some sense of the history of musical theatre and how vocal qualities and vocal delivery changed over time.

The cast of A Chorus of Disapproval *at their pre-performance warm-up at the Salisbury Playhouse in 1987.*

There are many debates about how and when the musical began, with many people agreeing that *The Black Crook* (1866) was the first American musical. At around the same time, and for some time into the twentieth century, operettas also continued, though again one might argue that comic opera was an earlier predecessor making the identification of a definite starting-point difficult. Operetta creators included Gilbert and Sullivan in Britain (*The Mikado*, *Pirates of Penzance* and *HMS Pinafore*), Franz Léhar (*The Merry Widow*) and Jacques Offenbach (*Orpheus in the Underworld*, *La Vie Parisienne* and *Tales of Hoffman*) in France, Sigmund Romberg (*The Student Prince*, *The Desert Song*) and Victor Herbert (*Babes in Toyland*, *Naughty Marietta*) who both moved from Europe to America. The works of all these composers would have been known in Europe and America. Other influences on the musical included music-hall, vaudeville, burlesque, spectacles, melodramas, pantomimes and minstrel shows.

During the first twenty years of the twentieth century these various forms began to coalesce into two strands of musical comedy that existed alongside the other popular performances. The first of these two strands was the early revue-style shows, the *Ziegfeld Follies* (which continued until 1927) and the *George*

Some Gilbert and Sullivan Songs

Songs you might sing from this period are predominantly from the Gilbert and Sullivan oeuvre, and include:

- 'I am a pirate king' (m);
- 'Poor wand'ring one' (f);
- 'I am the very model of a modern major-general' (m – patter);
- 'When a felon's not engaged in his employment' (or the policeman's song) (m – chorus);
- 'A wand'ring minstrel, I' (m);
- 'The sun whose rays are all ablaze' (f);
- 'Willow, tit willow' (m – character);
- 'Alone and yet alive' (f – character);
- 'As someday it may happen that a victim must be found' (or I've got a little list) (m – patter).

All these songs are from just two of the operettas, *The Mikado* and *Pirates of Penzance*, which leaves plenty more for you to explore and find much more material.

White Scandals (which continued sporadically until 1940), which contained spectacle, songs, dances and sketches. Many writers, composers and performers worked on these revues, who would later become stars in musical theatre. These included Irving Berlin, George and Ira Gershwin, Cole Porter, Jerome Kern, Fanny Brice, and Fred and Adele Astaire.

The other strand was shows that had a simple love story around which the rest of the production, including songs and dances, was loosely hung. These included the famous musical comedies at the Princess Theatre, which were much more intimate and had stories about relationships as an excuse for songs and dances, such as *Oh Boy!* with music by Jerome Kern. Other writers for the Princess Shows included Guy Bolton and P. G. Wodehouse. The types of performers at this stage were quite clearly defined and included hero and heroine, a young comedy couple and older performers singing predominantly character and comedy songs. The singing styles included using fast articulation in songs, at or around speech pitch and without a great musical range, for comedy and patter songs by the comedy characters, and lyrical ballads using longer phrases, greater melodic range and a classical approach to vocal technique by the hero and heroine. Almost without exception, heroines were sopranos and heroes were high baritones or tenors.

The next significant development was the production of *Show Boat* in 1927, which brought together Jerome Kern and Oscar Hammerstein who had written for the Princess shows. *Show Boat* was an adaptation of Edna Ferber's book of the same name that dealt with the serious theme of mixed-race relationships. It employed both black and white performers and attempted to ensure that each song provided a development of the plot or the character. There are two seemingly new ideas here, but the idea that songs should amplify character or plot was a development from the Princess shows and from operetta, while the use of a mixed-race cast was not new either. There had been a separate strand of African-American book musicals and shows that had developed since the end of slavery in America. *Clorindy, or the Origin of the Cakewalk* was the first to reach Broadway in 1898. Others followed, including *In Dahomey* in 1902, which toured to England, and *Shuffle Along* in 1921. Musicals continued to exist and there were mixed-race productions of, for example, *Uncle Tom's Cabin*. So *Show Boat* was not the first Broadway show to use black performers alongside white performers, but its popularity brought it, and the issues it raised, to the attention of a much wider public, and there was an attempt to introduce characters that were not the stereotypes used in musicals up to this point.

Despite a number of other musicals dealing with serious issues in the subsequent years, such as *Of Thee I Sing* (1931), *The Cradle will Rock* (1938), *Johnny Johnson* (1936), *Pal Joey* (1940) and the opera *Porgy and Bess* (1935), the majority of works during the next twenty years were light musical comedies. Musicals in these years included *Funny Face* (1927), *Girl Crazy* (1930), *Anything Goes* (1934), *On Your Toes* (1936) (which included the dramatic ballet 'Slaughter on Tenth Avenue') and *Babes in Arms* (1937). These provided escapist entertainment during the depression years and leading up to the Second World War.

The next important development in the history of musical theatre arose from the partnership of Richard Rodgers and Oscar Hammerstein, who in 1943 produced *Oklahoma!*. It had a strong book, adapted from Lynn Rigg's play *Green Grow the Lilacs*, but the advance in this musical is that not only are music and lyrics expected to contribute to the development of the plot and characters, but dance also contributes to the development and understanding of the story. Other works by Rodgers and Hammerstein include *Carousel* (1945), *South Pacific* (1949), *The King and I* (1951), and *The Sound of Music* (1959). In these works, what has become more pronounced is the importance of the continuous psychological development of a character (the same had been true of *Show Boat* and a number of other musicals in the intervening years). The difference is that rather than a

---

Songs by the Popular Song Composers of the 1920s–40s

Though not all from this period, songs by Berlin, the Gershwins, Porter or Kern are all standards in the musical-theatre repertoire, most of which can be sung interchangeably by men and women, and include such notable hits as:

- 'You're the top' (Cole Porter);
- 'My heart belongs to daddy' (Cole Porter);
- 'Smoke gets in your eyes' (Jerome Kern);
- 'S'Wonderful' (George and Ira Gershwin);
- 'Fascinatin' Rhythm' (George and Ira Gershwin);
- 'There's a somebody I'm longing to see' (George and Ira Gershwin);

and many more. You should browse song albums by these composers to find ballads, comedy songs and up-tempo numbers for your repertoire.

Songs from *Show Boat* include:
- 'Can't help loving that man' (f);
- 'Bill' (f);
- 'Ol' man river' (m);
- 'Life upon the wicked stage' (m & f – comedy).

---

musical-comedy plot or revue being the excuse for songs and dances that happened to be sung by the characters, songs in the more serious musical plays, or book musicals of writers such as Rodgers and Hammerstein, were seen as the opportunity for substantial character revelation, plot clarification or progression. This means that when you are preparing to sing these roles you need to have a much stronger sense of how the song fits into the plot, what it reveals about the character and how you, as the character, can maintain a psychological continuity between speech and singing.

75

This also impacts on the vocal colour and accent, which need to be consistently maintained from speech to song. However, the vocal ranges are still in line with those mentioned earlier: heroes and heroines have ballads and duets for soprano and tenor, while the comedy couple (Ado Annie and Will in *Oklahoma*) have the lower pitched, faster, comedy songs. This paralleling of characters as heroic and comic began to decline from this point on, though it is still apparent in many musicals; as, for example, in *Grease* where Sandy and Danny, the heroic couple, are mirrored by Rizzo and Kenickie, the down-to-earth or comic couple.

Alongside these musicals, and during the period from the 1940s to the end of the 1960s, there was a host of classic musicals – this is often referred to as the Golden Age of the musical. These musicals built on the idea of the musical play with a continuous development of characters, whose situations and relationships were worked out through dialogue and song. *Kiss Me Kate* (1948) is Cole Porter's masterpiece, based on the Shakespearean story of *The Taming of the Shrew* and contains two pairs of characters, and a double plot of an onstage story and the offstage antics of the performers, which each reflect the other. *Guys and Dolls* (1950), by Frank Loesser (and many collaborators) drawing on Damon Runyon's stories includes the Salvation Army 'doll' Sarah Brown and her gambler suitor Sky Masterson, and the low-comedy couple who have been engaged for fourteen years, Nathan Detroit and the hot box club singer Miss Adelaide. Also featured are excellent songs for the other gamblers and Salvation Army crowd, especially 'Sit down you're rocking the boat' and 'Luck be a lady'.

My Fair Lady (1956) by Lerner and Loewe, an adaptation of George Bernard Shaw's *Pygmalion*, is best known in the film version starring Audrey Hepburn and Rex Harrison. There are a number of songs in this musical that are suitable for character presentation rather than lyrical singing, though the young lover Freddie Eynsford Hill sings the beautiful 'On the street where you live' as a serenade to Eliza. 1957 saw the production of the

Songs from the 'Golden Age' of the Musical

These musicals contain a host of what are considered to be the classic songs of musical theatre including:

- 'People will say we're in love' (m & f – ballad) *Oklahoma!*
- 'I cain't say no' (f – character) *Oklahoma!*
- 'Some enchanted evening' (m & f – ballad) *South Pacific*
- 'I'm gonna wash that man right outta my hair' (f) *South Pacific*
- 'When I marry Mr Snow' (f – character ballad) *Carousel*
- 'You'll never walk alone' (m or f) *Carousel*
- 'Why can't you behave' (f) *Kiss Me Kate*
- 'Where is the life that late I led?' (m) *Kiss Me Kate*
- 'Brush up your Shakespeare' (m – comedy) *Kiss Me Kate*
- 'If I were a bell' (f) *Guys and Dolls*
- 'Adelaide's lament' (f – character) *Guys and Dolls*
- 'I'll know' (m & f – ballad) *Guys and Dolls*
- 'Just you wait' (f – character) *My Fair Lady*
- 'I've grown accustomed to her face' (m – character) *My Fair Lady*
- 'Something's Coming' (m) *West Side Story.*

immensely powerful *West Side Story* by Leonard Bernstein, which featured the young Stephen Sondheim as lyricist. This was a landmark in the development of dance in the musical, and again contained two couples among the principal characters: Tony and Maria (soprano and tenor); and Anita and Bernardo (mezzo and non-singer).

Other musicals of the period to consider include: *Gypsy* (1959), *Fiddler on the Roof* (1964), *Man of La Mancha* (1965), *Sweet Charity* (1966) and *Cabaret* (1966).

A substantial change occurred in the development of the musical in the 1960s. Alongside the continued development of book musicals throughout the 1960s and 1970s, rock and roll arrived in musical theatre. Since then, musicals have incorporated a range of popular styles that require different singing techniques. Arguably the first musical to incorporate rock and roll music was *Bye Bye Birdie* (1960). It took advantage of the popularity of this style of music and incorporated it in a story of a rock and roll star, though much of the music is in the style of musical comedy of the period. The same type of music is used in *Grease* (1978), best-known in its film version starring John Travolta and Olivia Newton-John, though at this later date the music is used to define the era of the 1950s, rather than as a sign of the current fashion. This tendency to use rock and roll as a designator of the hopes and dreams of the young of the 1950s continues in films such as *Footloose* and *Dancing in the Dark*. In other musicals, the popularity of the music is the excuse for compilation musicals focusing on the work of individual songwriters of the period, such as *Buddy: The Buddy Holly Story* (1989), *Five Guys Named Moe* (1992) and *Smokey Joe's Café* (1995) presenting the music of Lieber and Stoller.

Another group of rock musicals is led by *Hair* (1967). Here it is not the simple constructions of rock and roll, but the more challenging and aurally aggressive sounds of the developing rock and pop music of the period that illustrated this story of a young man during the Vietnam draft. Rock music, and its associations with urban disaffection, was an ideal signifier for a musical that represented the spirit of youth and free love, and that railed against authority. However, although the electronic instruments were amplified and the drums were featured as the rhythmic driver with a strong backbeat, the musical structures still stuck to a verse–chorus pattern reminiscent of mainstream musical theatre. *The Rocky Horror Show* (1974) again uses the associations of the mainstream population with various types of rock and pop music to signify characters; rock for the aliens, rock and roll for Eddie, Latin rhythms for the more sexual numbers and pop music for the earthlings. *Little Shop of Horrors* (1982) perhaps has more of a pop feel in most of its numbers, with the alien plant singing in a more urban rock idiom, but the construction of the music reflects a more mature appreciation and incorporation of popular music as an urban language in a gothic horror thriller. This strategy is brought up-to-date in *Rent* (1996), in which the four struggling young Bohemian artists (outsiders again) sing a score that is pervaded by a rock feel, though adapted for the theatre.

Jesus Christ Superstar (1971) and *Evita* (1978) (both by Tim Rice and Andrew Lloyd Webber) are both rock operas that are through-composed and first appeared as concept albums. *Tommy* (1969) is a rock musical that began as an album by The Who, and *Chess* (1984) also began as a concept album written by Benny Andersson and Bjorn Ulvaus (the writers in the pop group Abba). These musicals simply use rock music as a language rather than as a signifier of time, place and urban disaffection.

There are numerous other musicals – not least *Dreamgirls* (1981) that uses an amalgam of black music styles of the 1960s in a show that is thought to be based on the group The Supremes – that use popular musical styles to create a sense of time and place, and usually revolutionary, minority or disaffected youth culture. Other book musicals, such as *Les Miserables* (1980 in Paris, reworked for London 1985) and *Miss Saigon* (1989) incorporate rock and pop music into the language of the musical. Another group of musicals grew out of workshops and used popular musical styles as the language with which to communicate to a wide public. The most famous of these are *Hair* (1967), *Godspell* (1971) and *A Chorus Line* (1975).

The importance of the incorporation of popular styles into the musical is in the effect it has had on vocal production, and the loosening of the association of soprano and tenor vocal ranges with the leading characters: the young lovers. The style of singing in popular music is more earthy and less controlled, more overtly emotional and perceived as more 'authentic' or 'natural'. In musicals, however, the style of singing used in popular music has only influenced the vocal style and detached some previously common associations. It has allowed much greater ornamentation and variations of range, but when singing in musicals, the development of character, through both words and music, means that the words still need clear articulation and the emotional journey needs to be represented for the audience. There is therefore a clear difference

Songs from the Rock and Pop Repertoire

- 'I don't know how to love him' (f – ballad) *Jesus Christ Superstar*
- 'Gethsemane' (m) *Jesus Christ Superstar*
- 'Another suitcase in another hall' (f) *Evita*
- 'High flying, adored' (m) *Evita*
- 'Dentist' (m – comedy) *Little Shop of Horrors*
- 'Suddenly, Seymour' (f) *Little Shop of Horrors*
- 'Feed me' (m – the plant) *Little Shop of Horrors*
- 'There are worse things I could do' (f – character) *Grease*
- 'Greased lightnin'' (m) *Grease*
- 'And I am telling you I'm not going' (f) *Dreamgirls*
- 'When I first saw you' (m) *Dreamgirls*.

between singing in musicals and singing a pop song for recording or concert purposes. I will return to this in a subsequent chapter.

At the same time as musicals using contemporary pop and rock music were being introduced, other musicals continued to use what might be regarded as a musical-theatre convention. But even here there is an enormous range of music that requires different approaches to singing. Stephen Sondheim is perhaps the most important single composer of musical theatre, certainly in the second half of the century. He began writing lyrics for *West Side Story* and *Gypsy*, but went on to work with various book writers, creating both music and lyrics in a body of works over the past fifty years, including *Company* (1970), *Follies* (1971), *A Little Night Music* (1973), *Sweeney Todd* (1979), *Sunday in the Park with George* (1984), *Into the Woods* (1988) and *Assassins* (1991). The songs are immensely complicated

Songs by Stephen Sondheim

- 'Being alive' (m) *Company*
- 'Sorry-grateful' (m – ballad) *Company*
- 'Another hundred people' (f – up-tempo) *Company*
- 'I'm still here' (f – older character) *Follies*
- 'The 'God-why-don't-you-love me' blues' (m – character) *Follies*
- 'Losing my mind' (f – ballad) *Follies*
- 'On the steps of the palace' (f) *Into the Woods*
- 'Agony' (m – satire) *Into the Woods*
- 'Send in the clowns' (f – character) *A Little Night Music*
- 'Every day a little death' (f – ironic) *A Little Night Music*.

musical and textual compositions that often require a strong technique, a large vocal range, and exceptional articulation and clarity of rhythm, but they are also immensely detailed character studies that draw on a range of musical theatre styles and form a huge part of the contemporary repertoire.

More recent musicals that you might see or listen to include: *Honk* (1993), *Songs for a New World* (1997), *Parade* (1998), *Avenue Q* (2003) and *Floyd Collins* (1994).

Listening to a selection of this material will give you a sense of how the sound of the musical, and the sound of the voices in them, has changed in the course of the last century or so, especially since the 1960s.

7 INTERPRETING A SONG

As I said in the Introduction, singing in musicals uses particular styles of singing according to the musical style, but there are certain things that are constant across all types of musical-theatre performance in relation to methods of interpretation and representation of character for an audience. The most important feature is that the song is always sung by a character to express something and to add to the information the audience has. I will discuss this more fully in a later chapter but it is important always to be aware that there is an external focus for your expression of the song. One of the particular requirements of this is that you need to communicate with the audience and be aware of it, and of what it is seeing and hearing, even when you are not addressing the song directly to the audience. If you watch singers of a lot of popular music, you will find that they close their eyes and feel the emotion of the song for themselves and the audience is left on the outside looking in. In musical theatre it is very important that you keep your eyes open so that audience members can read your expression and can share the emotional development of the character and empathize with the character.

The second feature of musical-theatre singing is that there is always a context for the song. It is set in a scene within a story that is being interpreted, probably under the oversight and guidance of a director. This means that while you need to explore the potential interpretations of the song, its music and its lyrics, your interpretation must always be

Learning a Song

There are many songs that are widely known through performances on film or on recordings. However, when beginning to learn a new song, it is important to look at the song anew and try to forget how any particular singer has interpreted it before. This is particularly difficult if there is a version of the song, or a performance by an actor, that has made a role especially famous. There are examples of this in all the classic filmed musicals, with actors such as Joel Grey and Liza Minelli as the MC and Sally in Cabaret, or Natalie Wood and Chita Rivera as Maria and Anita (though Natalie Wood didn't sing) in *West Side Story*. Any re-interpretation of one of these famous songs is bound to be influenced by these earlier and possibly definitive versions. However, when learning a song you need to look again at the words and music, and make the interpretation your own.

moderated by the narrative situation, the character portrayal in the rest of the performance and the director's vision of the relationships of characters and situations. What I am suggesting below, therefore, is a method of learning and analysing a song and exploring potential interpretations, so that you have the tools to determine the most effective portrayal of character and situation through the musical material and in the circumstances of your production.

LEARNING A SONG

It's now time to think about how all that you have learned comes together in singing a song. There are many new things to think about at the same time as remembering what you have learned so far, so it's best to start with a solo song, and one that is relatively straightforward. You can consider some of the huge soliloquies, the comedy numbers and verbal ingenuity, the duets and group songs, and the rock and pop songs of the repertoire later, but for now, in order to put into practice the technical expertise you have developed, let's think about some of the classic ballads of musicals from the forties, fifties and sixties. As explained in Chapter 6, in this era are the great works by Rodgers and Hammerstein, including *Oklahoma!*, *Carousel* and *The Sound of Music*, as well as *West Side Story* (Bernstein and Sondheim), *Cabaret* (Kander and Ebb), *My Fair Lady* (Lerner and Loewe) and *Guys and Dolls* (Loesser), so you will have plenty to choose from no matter what your vocal range or whether you are male or female.

The hero's and heroine's roles are generally soprano and tenor in the musicals of this period, so to find something with a slightly smaller and lower vocal range, I've chosen to begin with a song from *Mack and Mabel* by Jerry Herman and Michael Stewart, which was published just after the target period in 1974. There is a book of vocal selections from *Mack and Mabel* available, and an original cast recording from 1974 with Bernadette Peters and Robert Preston, so you will be able to find the music and lyrics to 'I won't send roses'. The musical tells the story of the relationship between Mack Sennett, one of the pioneers of the film industry and a producer of comic 'two-reeler' films who subsequently also went on to make countless comic films, and Mabel Normand whom he discovered and who performed in his films. She became a comedy star, but left his studio because she wanted to perform dramatic roles and went on to star in other films before her early death in 1930.

Although this song is sung in the musical by Mack, it can be sung interchangeably by men and women outside the show, and is a useful song to use as an example, given its limited range and simple musical structures. It therefore provides an excellent vehicle for learning and developing your skills.

The reason I've chosen this song from *Mack and Mabel* is that you might not be quite so familiar with it; it is relatively slow and uncomplicated musically, while being a beautiful melody with emotionally complex lyrics. This will allow you time to think about your singing technique, as well as your interpretation, and to enjoy the song you're singing.

When looking at a new song, obviously you need to learn the words and the melody, but before you do that, just look at the words. With songs that are familiar there is a tendency to phrase words in certain ways, to give a sense of meaning that we have understood in general terms from other peoples' performances and

Watching and Listening to Performances

There are two clips on www.youtube.com of versions of 'I won't send roses' that you can find by searching for *Mack and Mabel*. The first is a concert version of this song by Michael Ball followed by 'Time heals everything' (which I will discuss in the next chapter) sung by Ruthie Henshall. These are different arrangements to those in the show, but give a flavour of the songs performed in a more flamboyant way for a concert. There is also an excerpt from 'I won't send roses' from the recent Newbury production of *Mack and Mabel* that went into London's West End, sung by David Soul. This is a more intimate performance as it is sung within the musical. Looking at, and listening to, these two performances and their different arrangements and performance styles is, itself, instructive.

from the melodic shape, and to breathe in places that either support that other interpretation or just wherever is easiest musically, without thinking about it at all. So, begin with 'I won't send roses', and write out the lyrics from the score, read them quietly to yourself, and begin to consider your interpretation.

If you know the melody of this song, it is likely that your natural inclination will be to separate 'I won't send roses' from 'or hold the door', and even more importantly, you might separate 'I won't remember' from 'which dress you wore'. I'm not suggesting that you must not breathe between these phrases if, when you look at the melody, it is imperative to do so, but that there is a sense of the meaning continuing through the line. The next two lines of the song also only make sense if you phrase them slightly against the expected musical pat-

tern. But read them through and work out the phrasing for yourself.

The next phase of development is to think about the detail of the words used in the song. The repeated use of the word 'roses' and the references to 'romance' and 'romantic' tell us something about how the character perceives himself as unromantic, even while throughout the song it becomes apparent that he knows what is expected within a romance. There is a lot in this song that draws parallels with 'I remember it well' from *Gigi*, in which the man remembers fondly but not well, while the assumption is that the woman remembers more clearly and correctly. In both cases, however, it is assumed that women need romance and the close attachment that Mack, here, says he is unable to make.

Two of the key phrases of the song occur towards the end of each verse. In the first verse, Mack uses the word 'love' without saying that he loves Mabel. He sings 'And should I love you, you would be the last to know', which obviously opens the question of what his feelings are for her, and links clearly with several other 'If I loved you' type songs from the repertoire, especially the song of that name from *Carousel* or 'People will say we're in love' from *Oklahoma!*. In the second verse, Mack's affection is demonstrated when he suggests that Mabel should leave because she deserves more than he will be able to give. These lines give the opportunity for the singer to create immense complexity in the song. Rather than a general feeling of sadness, Mack is demonstrating a deep love for Mabel, but he is also articulating how inept he feels at dealing with love or observing its conventions, and he admits to being self-obsessed. These facts, of course, make him far more attractive, as the self-deprecating man, exposing his vulnerability.

Putting the Song Together

There are several phases to the process of learning a song.

1. Explore the meaning and colours of the words, the phrases and sentences and potential interpretations.
2. Learn the melody without singing the words, so that you can address any technical difficulties, but also so that you can think about the shape of the melody, its emotional atmosphere and its dynamic shape.
3. Put the words and melody together and explore the possibilities for phrasing the song, based on your interpretation of the words and the shape of the melody.
4. Listen to the accompaniment while humming the melody, so that you understand the energy of the song and where the harmony is leading.
5. Think about how the song fits into its context, and what it needs to accomplish for the character and situation and feed that into your interpretation.

When you have a clear sense of the song lyrics and what you want to say through them, you should look at the melody (just the melody – not yet the harmony). Begin by singing the melody on your favourite vowel. This allows you to learn the melody and find where it sits in your voice. Don't add any ornamentation at this stage, simply sing the melody in the most simple and direct way. Make sure that the intonation of every note is absolutely clear, and that each phrase maintains a consistent vocal colour. So, for example, in the first line, the falling interval needs a controlled placing and the feeling of singing from above the note (with a head or mask of the face colour). This

avoids the feeling of landing with the volume and weight of chest sound on the very low note that might give the impression that the phrase is finished. Equally, with the rising intervals at the end of the first two lines, the tone colour needs to be consistent so that the notes don't suddenly stick out of the phrase.

As you sing through the melody you will begin to discover the musical phrasing, but you will also discover the shape of the verse. The verse begins with two similar lines in which only the last note alters. This makes that final note important, as attention is drawn to a single difference in a phrase of familiar repetition, so be aware of the importance of that note and consider its importance when adding the words. Equally you should be aware of other patterns of similarity and difference throughout the song. There is a change of pattern for the next two lines, which have a falling trajectory rather than a rising one, before an echo of the opening line (with a different falling interval) to complete the first half of the song. The second half of the song (from 'Forget my shoulder' and 'In me you'll find things') begins like a reprise of the opening – again a similarity – but the sequence

Daniel Hopkins maintaining a controlled delivery and direct address to the audience in 'Barbara' from **Starting Here Starting Now.**

quickly moves quite a lot higher and heads for the longest and highest note, the climax of the melody on 'is guaranteed' and 'that you deserve'. There is a second, less intense, musical echo of the climax as the melody falls and rises again to C, before the conclusion, which again echoes the opening.

The main difficulty in this song is likely to be that you begin to sing with too much chest colour to make the sound rounded and mellow, so that when you reach the climax of the song it feels extraordinarily high. If this is a problem for you, work out where in your voice you want to place the climax of the song and then maintain that colour as you begin the song again, mixing a little of the chest sound into the lower notes but maintaining the higher placing and control that is required later.

The second difficulty is likely to occur in the same place, as the phrase 'forgetting birthdays is guaranteed' covers the interval of a ninth. Because of the wide range in this phrase you may find you need a lot of support from the diaphragm and the abdominal muscles to control the breath for the leap. You will also need to make sure that the back of the throat is open and the palate lifted (the feeling of yawning and laughing silently). It is always useful to go back to an exercise that covers the range of the difficult phrase, so in this case, you should sing scales to a ninth covering the range of the phrase, and an exercise with a leap that mirrors that in the phrase. Then add vibrato as appropriate on the climactic note of the phrase.

The next difficulty is likely to be in maintaining the energy, since the climax is followed by a second, lesser moment a tone lower at the end of the next phrase, so the climax is not immediately released, but continues to need support. We will discuss the phrasing of this

Practising Difficult Moments

Wherever you find a technical demand being placed on your voice, devise an exercise based on those in the previous chapters, but that offers a chance to practise the particular technical difficulty. So if there is an interval leap that feels insecure, create an exercise using the vowels that you will have to sing in the song, and the same interval, but begin lower and work your way up to the level of the phrase in the song and beyond. Alternatively, you might need to reduce the size of the interval and practise increasing the intervallic range until you are comfortable with the leap that is required in the song. Equally, moments that require great agility or pace can be extracted and practised as separate exercises, so that when you arrive at that point in the song you are confident that your technique is able to cope.

section of the song when we put the words in, but for now, ensure that you can sustain the tone and the pitch effectively without strain. The final line of the second verse may cause difficulty because it is sustained as well as rising. As with the previous rising phrase, work out where you want the voice to be placed for the final, and highest, note and then maintain that colour and placement as you work backwards and lead up to it, making sure you have an open and released throat and sufficient support for the note.

Having become comfortable with the intonation of the melody on one vowel, try it on all the others, working out how to deal with any tricky technical problems that occur because of the change of vowel. For example, the higher notes will be placed differently and some people find them more difficult on 'oh' and 'oo' sounds. The 'ee' sound that has the tongue raised at the back needs to be as open as possible to create space for the higher notes. For this reason it is common practice to slightly adapt the vowel and use the more open sound 'I' as in 'ink', which helps to create the space needed but sounds like 'ee' when sustained. Throughout this exercise make sure that you are directing every sound to the hard palate for maximum resonance, and that you have not allowed tension to creep into any part of the mechanism.

When you are certain that you can sing the melody in a musical and tonally consistent way throughout, try one more exercise before adding the words. This time sing the melody on the vowels of the words that you are about to add. So the first line will be 'ah oh eh oh eh' using the first sound, 'ah', for the dipthong 'I'. The reason for this exercise is that you will discover which vowels you will be singing at the difficult moments, but also which vowels lead up to them, which can be quite important in practising the movement from one mouth shape to the next. The movement from one vowel to another should occur smoothly, but with a clear and energized articulation, so that the change of vowel doesn't sound sluggish or slurred, even though the pace of the song is slow. This is a really important point about slow songs; although the time you spend on each note may be longer than at the pace of speech, the speed of movement between words and the clarity of articulation should not become laboured. This exercise will also force you to sing different vowels while maintaining the tonal colour in a legato or smooth phrase.

Finally, and at long last, you should add the words to the melody after reminding yourself of all that you practised in bringing colour to the words. This is the point at which all the time you have spent working on the technical difficulties in the melody usually goes out of the window for a moment. But you must retain all that you have learnt so that both words and melody can work together in creating a consistent musical interpretation and expression of character for the audience.

PHRASING THE SONG

Now that you have mastered the technical difficulties of the melody and explored the colours and expression in the lyrics, you need to decide how to phrase the song, or decide where to breathe and where to sustain notes across the musical phrase. Sing through each phrase and, each time you come to a punctuation mark, decide whether you want to use it as a breathing place or just as punctuation. Remember, silence at a musical rest but without a breath being taken is also an option, and one too often ignored. It creates a wonderful feeling of suspension and anticipation.

You may decide on a breathing pattern and then find that the climax could be helped by a particular phrasing, so that you need to return to the earlier phrases leading up to the climax and refigure them. For example, I would take a breath in the first verse after 'too much in control' but then run the next two phrases together until 'gray, kid'. But in the second verse, the phrase is more likely to run from 'I'd be the first one' through to 'with me', before taking the breath while considering the next line, which puts the final nail in the coffin for Mabel by suggesting that Mack will never change.

Equally at the climax of the song, it is likely that you might choose to sing through the phrase 'Forgetting birthdays is guaranteed' with the same phrasing in the second verse. But what about the next phrase? In both verses it would seem sensible to run the two phrases together, but this may present difficulties in sustaining the sound on the 'C' of 'know' and 'go'. If you do take a breath between 'be' and 'the last' and its second verse equivalent, you will need to find a very good acting reason for it. I would suggest instead, that if you need an extra breath, in the first verse you could take a snatch breath at the comma after 'love you', while in the second verse you could reasonably argue the case for a breath after 'fighting chance'. The musical effect of singing the phrase through is impressive and more impassioned, but that may not be the effect you want to achieve at this point, or you may want to create that impression in one verse but not the other (usually the second would be the more impassioned). However, all these choices depend on your interpretation of the song, and your breath control.

This is the moment at which you see the point of separating the words and melody before reuniting them. The first two musical phrases of the song have a space between them that is enforced by the melody and yet the sentence continues. As an actor, and within the breath structure you have just decided on, you now have to work out how you are going to deal with this 'problem'. I put the word 'problem' in inverted commas, because the composer wrote it this way for a reason, and although you can never discern the reason in her or his mind, it is an opportunity for you to explore the potential interpretations offered by the musical phrasing. So, for example, that first phrase could be meditative and reflective leading to the pause within the line (between 'roses' and 'or'), or it could be that Mack is looking for examples to express the

Listening to the Accompaniment

Doubtless in your learning of the song you will have listened to several versions of it and become familiar with the accompaniment. But at this point it is helpful to listen to the accompaniment while humming the song.

- Listen to the rhythm of the accompaniment and whether it drives the song or rests quietly, whether it follows the singer or maintains a constant tempo.
- Listen too, to the places at which there are interesting or unexpected harmonies and think about what these require of the melody and the singer.
- Think about the atmosphere the accompaniment creates and decide how the melody and the words relate to that atmosphere.

things he is not good at. Either of these interpretations is possible, and the interpretation you choose will depend on your own reading of the song and the character and how the song is framed in the production. The point is that it is your job as an actor to explore the potential interpretations and work out what is consistent with the music and lyrics, and at the same time best expresses the ideas and emotions you want to portray through the song.

In the same way that the music enforces a word length and a pace on the performance, it also enforces a dynamic shape (which will be discussed more fully in the next chapter), with a softer start, a more rhythmic second section, a climax followed by an echo and a resolution to the starting pace and pitch. This gives an arch-like structure with a climax about two-

Mary Lincoln working with the accompaniment when singing 'My ship' by Kurt Weill in Has Anybody Seen my Tiddler? *Falmouth Arts Centre (1997).*

The musical accompaniment also creates an atmosphere that can't be ignored in your interpretation. Listening to the accompaniment will help you to understand the atmosphere or mood of the piece and any changes that are suggested by unusual or unexpected harmonies, key changes and so on. The accompaniment to 'I won't send roses' is quite economical, it maintains a steady pace so that the singer can delay or advance words in a phrase (a *colla voce* accompaniment

---

Other Songs You Might Choose at this Stage

- 'I've never been in love before' from *Guys and Dolls* (in the score this song is arranged in two keys: the first lower version for male voice, followed by the higher version for female voices, which gives you two options for your practice)
- 'I'll know' from *Guys and Dolls* (this too is written in two keys for male and female voices)
- 'If I were a bell' sung by Sarah in *Guys and Dolls*
- 'Why should I wake up' sung by Cliff in the stage version of *Cabaret*
- 'Married' sung by Herr Schultz and Frau Schnieder in the stage version of *Cabaret* also has two keys, and is a useful song if you expect to play older characters
- 'On the street where you live' sung by Freddie in *My Fair Lady*.

  Alternatively, you might try some classic songs that are not directly related to any show, but were used as film themes, such as:
- 'Two sleepy people' by Frank Loesser and Hoagy Carmichael
- 'Moon River' by Johnny Mercer and Henry Mancini
- 'Alfie' by Hal David and Burt Bacharach.

---

thirds of the way through the song, sometimes followed by a big finish, but at other times, by a return to the mood of the start. This shape is extremely common in lyrical ballads, and within musicals the arch-like structure is useful as the song can then grow out of the scene and return to speech without too much disruption. The big finish is likely to lead to applause, which would interrupt the scene, so choosing which ending you will perform is affected by its placement, either in a concert, when you are likely to want applause, or in a scene, when you may want to continue the scene and not break the mood.

would alter pace with the singer, while a rhythmic one like this allows the singer to pull away from and back to the tempo). It also supports the climactic moments with more complex harmonies. In particular, listen to the change of harmony that occurs under the sustained climactic notes at the words 'the last to know', and listen to the resolution or sense of closure that it suggests before the restatement of the theme. Elements of interpretation are implied in the musical accompaniment, and you need to be fully aware of it.

As you have now discovered, there is an awful lot to take into consideration when beginning to learn a song; this is why singers talk about the time it takes to 'sing a song into their voice'. It takes a while to discover how the song sits in your vocal range, how you can fashion the solution to any technical difficul-ties into an artistic interpretation and how you interpret the combination of materials the composer and lyricist have created into a musical and coherent expression that says what you want it to say at that point in the performance.

Obviously the strategies suggested using this example can be used to learn any other song. However, it is wise to begin with songs that cover a fairly limited vocal range, that are not too fast and that encourage you to sing melodic lines, rather than articulating the words of faster and comic songs, and that require you to think about breath patterns and phrasing. The important thing is to find a small number of songs that you really enjoy singing so that you can develop your technical skills and practise the process of learning and interpreting a new song.

8   SHAPING A SONG

Part of the process of learning a song, discussed in the last chapter, was the analysis of the musical shape of the song to discover where the climax of the song lies, how the song starts and finishes, and what the emotional range of the song should be. As we saw, 'I won't send roses' has a dynamic shape with a climax about two-thirds of the way through the first verse, with a repetition in the second verse that would consequently lead to a more intense climax a short way before the end of the song. There was the possibility of two endings, low in the first verse as the song continues, and high in the second, which is likely to generate applause.

In this chapter I'm going to look at some other possible dynamic shapes for songs and consider the issues they raise for the singer, how they affect interpretation and the sorts of responses they inspire from the audience. The dynamic shape of a song is partly dependent on the structure of the song. The structure of the song is basically the pattern of the musical material; its repeated sections, verse structure, bridge material (new musical ideas presented only once), introduction and coda (end section).

Common Structures in Popular Songs

The most common structures for popular songs are the following:

1. ABABAB. This is a verse and chorus structure, where the same musical material is repeated with different lyrics in each verse and often the same lyrics in the refrain.
2. AABA. In this structure, the A section is usually eight bars long, with a slightly varied repetition. The B section is a contrasting section that usually contains the climax, followed by a return to the mood of the start with a varied ending and possibly more verses following the same pattern. This was the most common format in the classic period and can be seen in 'I won't send roses' in Chapter 7.
3. Some combination of repeated sections and new material, such as ABABCAB, where C is a new bridge section before the final reprise. 'Something's coming' is one of these strange combinations that doesn't quite follow any pattern and will be discussed below.

These structures allow the audience to recognize the melody of different parts of the song and become familiar with the patterns.

DYNAMIC SHAPES

The dynamic shapes of songs can vary widely in more complex songs such as the soliloquies of Billy in *Carousel* or Sweeney and the Judge, both in *Sweeney Todd*, but there are three common shapes that you will be familiar with from listening to many songs. The first is the shape attached to a verse/chorus structure, where there is a climax about two-thirds of the way through each verse/chorus. 'Time heals everything' from *Mack and Mabel* falls into this category and will be discussed below.

There are similarities between the shape of a repeating verse structure that also builds to a big finish and the slow build. The slow build contains quite a lot of repeated musical material, but is characterized by a gradual increase in volume and pitch throughout the whole song, so that the overall dynamic shape is one of a gradual build in pitch and volume from the beginning to the end of the song. These are the big applause songs sung by singers such as Liza Minnelli and Shirley Bassey, such as 'Maybe this time' from the film version of *Cabaret* and 'New York, New York', from the musical of that name. I will discuss 'Maybe this time' below.

The arch-shape uses a variety of musical structures, but there is likely to be a gradual rise in pitch and volume to a central section of the song for the climax, followed by a return to the pitch and volume of the start of the song. There is also often new material in the centre

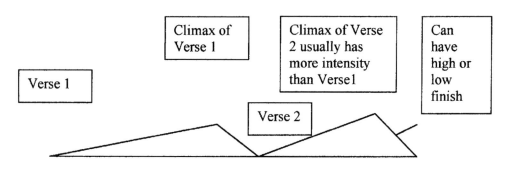

The dynamic shape of some songs with verse/chorus structure.

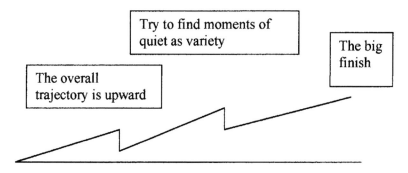

Figure 9 – The long, slow build.

of the song and sometimes a mirroring of the shape (the material itself is not reflected and so is not presented backwards as in the retrograde sections of serial music). An example would be the structure ABCBA, where B contains the same material as the earlier B section, or ABCB1A1 in which the material in B1 is a developed or altered but identifiably similar version of the material in B.

This is a useful shape in musical theatre because it can appear that the song is a dream-like fantasy outside the time and place of the story, since the musical material is similar at the beginning and end. It is used in both Tony's songs in *West Side Story* (1957) and in 'On the steps of the palace' from *Into the Woods*, which will be discussed in a later chapter. I will discuss one of the *West Side Story* songs, 'Something's coming', below.

Representing Emotion

In order to learn the song, you should go through the same process as that described above of learning the words as an actor, learning the melody using only vowel sounds and practising any technical difficulties, then putting the song together and crafting the dynamic shape of the piece to express your interpretation of the song. In all songs you need to make sure that you have mastered the technical demands of the music before focusing on interpretation. There is a sense in which your brain needs to be split in two, so that part of your brain is dealing with emotion, while, even in performance, part of your brain is cool and collected and focusing on the technical aspects of the delivery. If you become totally involved in the music or the emotion of a song it is likely that the technique will suffer, leading to tension and forcing of the sound and, ultimately, damage to the voice. It is important, therefore, to remember that a singer re-creates the emotions and interpretation of a song so that the audience perceives the emotions, rather than the singer allowing the emotion to take over the performance.

WORKING ON SOME EXAMPLES

Time Heals Everything

'Time heals everything', also from *Mack and Mabel*, is a song with an AABA structure in each of two verses. Each of the repeated verses is musically identical until the final phrase

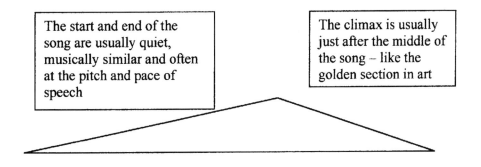

> The start and end of the song are usually quiet, musically similar and often at the pitch and pace of speech

> The climax is usually just after the middle of the song – like the golden section in art

Figure 10 – Arch shape.

Developing the Shape of the Song

There are a number of stages to developing the dynamic shape of a song.

1. Analyse the structure of the song and note where repetitions and climaxes occur.
2. Explore how this fits with your interpretation of the song and decide where you want to sing at louder or softer volumes, and whether those changes are sudden or gradual.
3. Work out the phrasing and breathing pattern that suits your voice and allows you to support the notes and words you have decided are important, but that also suits the character and the situation.
4. Make sure you understand the context of the song in the show, as well as the style of singing for the period and for the production.
5. If you have a choice of key for the song, work with your musical director to find the optimum place in your voice for the climactic impassioned notes, then make sure that singing at that pitch doesn't affect your delivery of any other part of the song. If there is no choice then you need to develop the technique to produce the sounds you want at the pitch required.
6. Find all the moments in the song at which you can change the vocal colour so that there is a variety of emotion and tone quality rather than a single emotion and vocal tone that will lead to a predictable climax.

- Learn the song as described in Chapter 7.
- Do some research into the character and situation in the plot.
- Explore the historical period and style of the song.
- Discuss what the director and musical director want from the song in your production.
- Analyse the structure of the song and identify the repeated musical material, the climaxes, any musical and verbal motifs and the dynamic shape of the song.

Now you feel that you have a sense of the song, its context and its purpose, you can start working on your interpretation of it.

Sing the song through at a range of pitches before concentrating on the final two lines of the song, 'time heals everything but loving you' in the second verse. You need to be able to sing the final three E flats on the vowels 'Oh, I, Oo' at full volume and sustained. The indications in the score suggest that the singer should pause on the final part of the word 'loving', and take a breath between 'loving' and 'you' in the second verse (the tramlines in the score indicate a break that is longer than would be expected in strict rhythm). Although it seems counter-intuitive to work out the song backwards, you need to know where you're going to arrive at before you can decide how to get there. If the final notes have a particular tone colour, you need to work out how to prepare for them so that they don't sound different to the rest of the song; there is nothing worse than the voice slipping over a break at the climax of the song. You will also need to plan your breathing in this line; common practice is to breathe after 'everything'.

So now you have decided on the tone colour for the final phrase, sing into it from the previous phrase, which is pitched at almost the

with the high finish (as shown in the diagram on page 90). So your task in interpreting the song is to find tonal and emotional differences between sections that are musically similar, in order to develop an appropriate dynamic shape and a complex interpretation.

same level of height and intensity. Now go back to the lower 'Time heals everything' that requires a leap of a seventh between the repetition of the words. Use the strategies suggested in the work on 'I won't send roses' to practise the interval leap while retaining a consistent tone colour. This is your maximum volume and intensity, and this is the most impassioned sound you are going to make in this song, as it should be at the climax of the song, so working backwards again, you need to discover how to sing the whole song (both verses) without arriving at that point of intensity too early.

There is a natural crescendo (build) in the first half of the song, as the intervals at the start of each phrase are larger and leap to ever higher notes. However, the words 'And one fine morning the hurt will end' have a lower pitched melody and allow a momentary respite from the pain and the increasing volume. The second half of the song naturally begins with more urgency than the first half (but remember you still have the second verse, so don't give the game away yet). The next opportunity to vary the colour and emotion is during the quaver pattern of 'Tuesday, Thursday' and so on. Here each word or phrase needs an individual thought and the whole phrase needs its own small crescendo as the character becomes more and more desperate for relief. In order to achieve this, there needs to be a dip in intensity at the start of the phrase. The same process occurs in the next lines; if there is a sense of relief and calmness on the first delivery of the title line you will be able to alter the intention for the second iteration. In the first verse, the final phrase falls back down, so take this opportunity to reduce the volume though you will need to maintain the intensity.

There is an instrumental section at the start of the second verse, so take this opportunity to become calmer and more reflective, so that the distance from quiet to loud, relaxed to intense, over the course of the final half-verse is as wide as possible. Also, continue to look for new interpretations for each word, phrase and line, while not detracting from the shape of the whole song. Finally, when you reach the climax, gratification will have been delayed so long that there is a sense of relief for the listener in the resolution of the song as a full-bodied vocal cry, which is likely to lead to rapturous applause.

Maybe This Time

'Maybe this time' is available in a book of vocal selections from *Cabaret*, which contains a selection of songs from the film version. It has a slow continuous build through the song, and is therefore harder to sing than 'Time heals everything' because its melody rises more consistently, and it therefore offers fewer opportunities to pull back or change the emotional colour. However, unless you find those moments of change, the song can become one-dimensional and boring, and the attempt to keep getting louder can cause forcing of the voice.

There are a number of problems specific to songs that have a consistent slow build, whether or not you would define them as torch songs. The principal of these is that singers tend to begin at too high an emotional pitch and arrive at too loud a volume too soon in the song. In the same way that, in 'I won't send roses' and 'Time heals everything', you found the climax of the song and worked out any breathing problems so that the climax was effective, in these songs you need to discover where you want to arrive at by the end of the

93

Torch Songs

Torch songs are sung by the lover who continues to carry a torch for a love that is over. However, the term is also used sometimes for songs about love that have a slow build throughout. They begin at a low pitch and quietly and gradually rise to a high-pitched and loud climax, which is the end of the song. Examples of songs that have this shape are 'Maybe this time' from *Cabaret* or the theme tune from *New York, New York*. Songs in this category with a soul influence include 'And I am telling you I'm not going' from *Dreamgirls* in which the increased intensity is expressed through increased volume and ornamentation with less concentration on the rise in pitch, though it is still an important factor. The third element in this type of song is the use of a belt or cry sound in the voice that demonstrates the impassioned feelings of the character.

song, and then explore how you are going to get there without giving away your vocal climax too early.

The song consists of three sections that each begin with similar material but develop differently and so the structure might be identified as A, A1, A2. A is from the start until 'and the time before'. A1 uses a similar melody but develops differently from the third line, ending at 'maybe this time I'll win' (the first time it's sung). A2 comprises similar material to A1 but transposed up a semitone, and begins at 'Everybody loves a winner' and runs to the end of the song. Having identified this structure it is already possible to find moments when the pitch falls, which are mostly at the beginning of each new section, so that a new

rising sequence can begin at each restatement of the opening material. These moments provide the most obvious opportunities for changes in vocal colour and for reducing the volume (but not the intensity) and starting a new build.

The short phrases, especially at the lower pitches, allow opportunities for a delivery very close to that of speech, while the higher pitched phrases at times might be carried over, linking two appropriate phrases to increase the emotional intensity. Equally, and without joining two phrases, you might consider the length of the sustained notes at the end of each phrase. So, for example, you might decide to shorten the last note of the phrase 'nobody loved me', but you might sustain the note and crescendo on the last note of the phrase for the joyfulness of 'something's bound to begin' into 'it's got to happen'. In this way you can alter the intensity by moving closer to singing or to speaking.

The start of the song is extremely important in introducing a range of emotions so that the song doesn't begin too loud. There is optimism in the opening lines, coloured by the vulnerability of 'for the first time he won't hurry away' and later 'not a loser anymore'. Achieving this sort of vulnerability at the start introduces the potential for a complex characterization and for avoiding the difficulty of just getting louder and louder. There are also opportunities to change the mood or intensity later in the song, introducing, for example, wryness at 'everybody loves a winner, so nobody loved me'. You might then continue with a moment of reflection for the line beginning 'Lady peaceful', before reasserting with determination that 'all the odds are in my favour' and so on. The interpretation of the song relies on a constant juxtaposition

Beverley Klein performing the big finish in Starting Here, Starting Now, *St Luke's Theatre Exeter (1997).*

between awareness of vulnerability, and determination and excitement about the current love affair and its future potential.

These sorts of considerations are important in all songs to find the most interesting shape and colour for the interpretation of the song, but they are particularly essential to songs whose musical shape and structure tends to suggest a consistent pattern that might need resisting in the singer's interpretation.

Something's Coming

'Something's coming', sung by Tony in *West Side Story*, has the arch-like structure mentioned above. The song happens early in the plot of *West Side Story*. In the scene preceding it, Riff and Tony's relationship has been established, but Tony's excitement about moving forward into a new phase of his life is also made clear. During the song the accompani-

Tony and Maria rehearsing lines of West Side Story *on the tour bus of the European tour, December 1986–87.*

ment also maintains the pulse of excitement (possibly Tony's racing heart) throughout, maintaining a drive underneath even the most lyrical sections of the melody.

95

It begins and ends with similar musical material and at a similar dynamic and pitch level so that the song appears to grow out of a plot situation and emotional atmosphere and fall back into it. The accompaniment contributes to this suggestion of how the song might be interpreted; at the start because it fades in under Riff's last sentence, and at the end because it fades again as the scene changes. This suggests the volume of the opening vocal lines, which grow from the end of the scene as a breath of possibility rather than leaping in to express a new emotion. This means that the song appears to the audience like a fantasy outside the linear time of the story. This allows the performer to explore aspects of the character that contribute to the story, but that wouldn't be possible within a totally realistic portrayal.

Obviously, you need to begin working on 'Something's coming' by learning the song in the same way as usual. But with this song, look closely at the dynamic markings in the score. These give you a lot of information about the dynamic shape of the song. The opening two phrases are marked 'pp' and are sustained over a rhythmic accompaniment, so the music creates the excitement, while the voice creates a quiet, sustained, possibly thoughtful moment of discovery. The next section is close to the pitch of speech, but is outside the rhythmic patterning of speech. Here the rhythm and the silent rests contribute to the feeling of breathless excitement leading to a crescendo on the sustained note and the loud release of the short 2/4 section. Immediately on the word 'rose' there is a diminuendo and the excitement is pulled back and internalized again. This pattern of barely contained excitement expressed through quiet moments of questioning and moments of joy-

Dynamic Markings

Dynamic markings on the score are indications given by the composer about the volume, intensity and pace at which s/he wants the song to be sung. The following are some of the most common:

p – piano – quietly;
pp – pianissimo – very quietly;
f – forte – loudly;
ff – fortissimo – very loudly;
mf or mp – mezzo-forte or mezzo-piano – quite loudly or quite softly;
dim – diminuendo – getting softer, sometimes signified by $\textgreater\!\!\!=$

cresc – crescendo – getting louder, sometimes signified by $=\!\!\!\textless$

> – an accent marking;
rit – ritardando – pull back the pace (generally for short time – a phrase or section);
rall – rallentando – getting slower;
accel – accelerando – getting faster;
a tempo – return to the original pace;
colla voce – literally with the voice – the singer is free to interpret the words at a pace and rhythmic pattern closer to speech and the accompaniment will follow.

ful release characterizes the first part of the song. At the words 'around the corner' the mood changes as the pitch of the song rises and the words are much more sustained. This is the moment of absolute certainty that the dream will appear; the character is painting a picture of his clear and joyful vision of the future. It also contains the highest notes yet on 'whistling down the river', which mark the climax of the song before the pitch and volume decrease again.

Shaping a Song

- Identify the structure of the song.
- Find the climaxes and discover how to work towards them, but also how to provide contrast to them.
- Vary the colour, emotion, atmosphere, volume, intensity and mood as much as is possible within the confines of the plot, character and situation.
- Reconsider the phrasing and interpretation in light of what you have now discovered about the song.

The range between loud and soft gets even greater as Tony vacillates between not daring to suggest that his dreams will come true and his joyful calling for his life to begin. However, the echo of the climax, 'the air is humming', is not so loud or externalised, allowing him to feel the certain proximity of his dream becoming reality. Finally, the dynamic markings and the musical material returns to echo the start, and the moment fades.

There is a second layer of interpretation being suggested here that relies on awareness of the context of the song, its accompaniment, its musical and lyrical structure, its dynamic shape and its potential to provide vocal and musical climaxes. So as I said earlier, singing in musical theatre relies on a combination of being emotionally engaged and aware in the moment of singing the song, but at the same time distanced so that you can retain an awareness of technique and structure. This is so that the emotion, atmosphere and plot are represented to the audience in ways that allow the audience to empathize with the character. This is different from singing for yourself. In musical theatre you need to allow or even encourage the audience to empathize with the character, and to do this you need to understand the structures and how to represent situations and characters, rather than simply how to feel them for yourself.

9 Exploring the Character

Ispoke above about the separation of performer and character that is required in performing musical-theatre songs, so that the technical aspects of the song and the interpretation are controlled by the performer, while the character is on an emotional or intellectual journey of discovery. This is a strange separation of the self in performance, but it is essential to the professional delivery of a performance in a musical. The performer needs to have an understanding, not only of the song itself but what it needs to accomplish in its context, and what sort of response it needs to inspire in its audience. At the same time, the character has to appear to be innocent of such planning and to maintain a realistic approach to the development of the narrative.

If you stop for a minute and try to concentrate on something you will discover that your brain doesn't function in a linear fashion but dashes off in many different directions. Equally, if you set yourself a problem to solve, your brain will keep introducing new aspects of the problem rather than developing a single strand of argument. That is why many people rely on writing lists of pros and cons to make decisions. If you listen to other peoples' conversations you will discover that they veer off at tangents, and refer to a host of different experiences and situations. This process is revealed directly in the lyrics of some songs by Sondheim or Maltby and Shire such as 'Crossword puzzle' or 'On the steps of the palace' (discussed below). However, it is the representation of this sense of the brain as active and constantly in motion, changing mood, having new ideas, that creates a feeling of life and energy in all songs, and there are strategies below for developing the skill of re-creating this energy in performance.

REVEALING THE CHARACTER'S JOURNEY

There is an exercise that I have used myself and I have seen used in workshops on singing in musical theatre. It has slight variations, but is designed to encourage you to treat the song as a process of discovery for the character, even while you, as the singer, maintain a sense of awareness and technique outside the character and control the journey through the song that is undertaken by the character.

The basic premise of the exercise is that the character undertakes a journey through a song, during which new thoughts occur to her/him constantly, and during which she/he makes decisions and choices. The character might refer to memories or situations that give information to the audience, but which have an emotional charge for the character. All of these thought processes need to be within the control of the performer, but represented as fresh and original to the audience. The character needs to appear to speak with truth and to have thoughts and emotions in the moment, despite the pre-planning and re-creation that is required by the production.

In my version of this exercise I discuss the song and the character's journey through it with the student, and we explore, by speaking and singing the song, where changes occur for the character. This is then transferred to the rehearsal space where the performer needs to create enough physical signs of change in their voice, face, eyes, body language and gesture that other people can perceive the exact moments of change during the journey of the song. In other versions of the exercise I have seen singers click their fingers, clap or raise their hand whenever there is a change of thought as they progress through the song. These physical gestures are particularly useful when singing with other characters, as the hearer of the song is then aware of the change in thought process (though they should also register it from the performance) and is therefore able to respond appropriately.

What these exercises have in common is the recognition that a song is not a reflection of a single emotional state, but that emotional changes occur during it that reveal the character to the audience. This fact has already been established to some extent during the work on 'Maybe this time' in the previous chapter, where the importance of changes of thought was used to help create the dynamic shape and build the song's climax. Now we're developing this strategy so that a song is seen

---

Some Questions to Think About

- Who is the character singing to and what do they reveal? This question explores the relationships between people onstage at the time of the song.
- Who is the performer singing for? This question explores the relationship between performer and any audiences, which may include other characters onstage.
- Why is the character singing? This question begins to explore the structure of the scene and the whole performance and to understand the stimulus that has led to song.
- Are there any other characters singing or speaking? Here again you are encouraged to explore relationships, but particularly to think about who speaks and who sings, at what points, and why.
- What is the character saying? What the character is saying might be different to what the performer wants the audience to perceive; characters can lie to others or deceive themselves, and the singer needs to be aware of both layers.
- What is the song saying? This question attempts to understand what the audience might perceive within the song in relation to the character, the scene and the story.

---

within a context that is both narrative, developing the song and the character within the story, and at the same time part of a production, exploring the song's function within the performance as a whole.

The questions listed above and the exercise for changing thoughts will be used in three examples below to demonstrate their effect in understanding the function of a song, both in terms of the character and for the performer in a production. In practice, you are likely to use both of these exercises (or very similar ones) in the course of learning a song for a performance, as you need to understand both the journey of the character and the function of the song.

The three songs are chosen from musicals from two different time periods. The first is 'People will say we're in love' from *Oklahoma!* by Rodgers and Hammerstein (1943) in which both Curly and Laurey dissemble about their love for each other. The second and third are both by Stephen Sondheim; there are two because one is for a man and one for a woman, though it is worth reading about both as they raise different issues and are examples of the two different exercises. They are 'Being alive' from *Company* (1970) sung by Robert, the 'hero' at the end of the show, and 'On the steps of the palace' sung by Cinderella on her way home from the ball towards the end of Act One of *Into the Woods* (1987).

WORKING THROUGH SOME EXAMPLES

People Will Say We're in Love

'People will say we're in love' is number 12 in the vocal score of *Oklahoma!* but it is also widely available in collections of musical-theatre songs. In addition, most Rodgers and Hammerstein scores are likely to be available through your local library. There are also numerous versions performed by amateur companies available on YouTube, as well as a jazz version that accompanies shots of Buffy and Spike falling in love taken from *Buffy the Vampire Slayer*. The song occurs about two-thirds of the way through the first act of the musical after Laurey has agreed to go to the

social with Judd Fry. Curly, the hero, is jealous but tries to hide it. Laurey and Curly have a flirtatious scene in which each denies being in love with the other, despite the flirtation that is plainly going on between them. At the end of the scene there is a short exchange as follows:

> Laurey: Most of them say that you're stuck on me!
> Curly: Can't imagine how these ugly rumors start.
> Laurey: Me neither.

Then Laurey sings. The first verse is an exchange between the two characters in which Laurey suggests a strategy for stopping the gossip that both acknowledge is going on about them and their possible relationship. The refrain is sung first by Laurey then Curly sings a verse and refrain.

The verse follows on directly from the scene in a conversational style, beginning with a question for each character. The pace of delivery is not far removed from that of speech, though the pitch is significantly higher. This means that the sense of a continued conversation from the spoken section is possible, and in fact desirable in what is sometimes referred to as the first integrated musical. The task for the performers, therefore, is to make the transition from speech to song as smooth as possible by maintaining the style and tone colour from speech to song. Laurey then introduces the refrain as 'a practical list of "don'ts" for you'. The task for the performer from then onwards is to find variety in the many things that the lovers shouldn't do if they are to scotch the rumours that they are in love, but also to discover the journey that the song creates for the characters so that they are in a changed position at the end. The premise of the song is that they are revealing all the things they each do that demonstrate their growing affection. It is this sense of togetherness and agreement that can be used to counter the lyrical suggestions that they are not in love. So here is an example of a song in which the characters begin by dissembling, but reveal their feelings through the heightened emotion of song.

There are three sections in the refrain. Each section concludes with the line 'People will say we're in love', which acts as a recognizable motif. The first and second sections are almost the same melodically. The third is different; it is musically more complex, as it modulates through other keys and finishes much higher, as the climax of the verse. However, it still ends

with the title line resolving back to the D major home key ready to move to A for the second verse and D for the refrain, so there is a sense of resolution.

As with earlier songs, you need to learn the song and decide on an appropriate phrasing pattern that allows you to breathe to support the musical line and the sense of the words. Then try the 'changing thoughts' exercise. Certainly there is likely to be a change of thought for most new lines; however, there are also changes of tack so that groups of lines have a similar direction revealing the journey of the song. I would suggest that the first line by Laurey is coquettish, since Curly hasn't been seen throwing any bouquets. But then

Mary Lincoln singing George Gershwin's 'The Lorelei', in which the true nature of the Lorelei is gradually revealed in the course of the song.

she thinks of a new suggestion for her list, which is more difficult for Curly since he gets on well with Aunt Eller; 'Don't please my folks too much'. The next suggestion is even more down-to-earth and refers to the lively character of the exchange they have just had by suggesting that he shouldn't laugh at her jokes and should tone down his pleasure in her company. The motif follows, here perhaps giving a warning of what might happen if he continues doing these things. However, this group of phrases is quite down-to-earth, possibly colloquial and certainly jokey and good-humoured.

The next group begins in the same half-joking style as she warns him against the demonstrable signs of love: sighing and gazing at her. But the line continues as she acknowledges that she does the same in the lines: 'your sighs are so like mine, your eyes mustn't glow like mine'. These phrases allow a completely different mood to enter as Laurey acknowledges that they have similar feelings of love for each other. In the second verse at the same place Curly also reveals his feelings, though to a lesser extent, with the line 'your hand feels so grand in mine'.

In the third section, both openly admit that they enjoy being together: Laurey by calling Curly 'Sweetheart', and in the second refrain, Curly talks about the two of them dancing 'Till the stars fade from above' and that that is 'alright with me'.

So through each refrain there is a process of revelation of the true state of their feelings for each other. They continue to sing the motif line 'People will say we're in love' but it has changed from something that they are joking about and trying to avoid, to something they are acknowledging as true. This is the journey for each character in the song, so that by the end of the song the scene can continue in a totally different vein.

It is this larger scale process of discovering the journey of the song, as well as the meanings and associations of the lyrics, that is the reason for the exercises suggested above.

Being Alive

'Being alive' is an articulation of the process of reasoning, as the hero, Robert, first of all explores the situation in marriage as the feeling of being smothered or needed too much, which is pretty much the theme of the musical *Company* in which it is featured as the final song. In the first verse he sings 'Someone to hold you too close, Someone to hurt you too deep, Someone to sit in your chair, to ruin your sleep'. However, the transition to the second verse switches the words as Robert realizes that, while relationships are never perfect and require compromise, they are now something he feels he wants and needs to embrace. So he now sings 'Somebody hold me too close, Somebody hurt me too deep, Somebody sit in my chair and ruin my sleep and make me aware of being alive'. This very slight alteration in the lyrics marks an immense shift in the position of the character as he now declares his desire for a partner, even though the entire show has demonstrated the inadequacies of other peoples' marriages and of Robert's own limited capacity for forming successful loving relationships.

However, arguments about the ending of *Company* and the ambiguity it opens up for its principal character aside, I'm going to look here at the version of 'Being alive' that is published in *The Stephen Sondheim Songbook* (1979) and the vocal selections from the score (published in 1996), as these are more widely available than the complete vocal score. These are also the versions that are most often used in auditions or concert performances outside the show, as they present a single perspective rather than the change of perspective through the intervention of other people encompassed in the show version. This version of the song has a structure that follows the pattern A A1 B A2 (where B is developed from the extended ending of A), and takes the dynamic shape of a slow build with the climax at the end of the song after almost reaching the climax at the end of section B.

In the course of the song the singer vacillates between the positive and the negative aspects of being in a close relationship. It is the variety of the images on either side of this divide that provide the emotional range and argument of this song. This is epitomized in such lines as 'Somebody... put me through hell and give me support for being alive'. So at the local level there is change within individual lines of the song, but there is also an overriding narrative in the song. This moves from a statement of desiring that somebody should be in his life, in the first part of the song, to the very clear statement 'but alone is alone, not alive', which represents a new certainty about what he has discovered and how he wants his life to proceed. This is then followed by the restatement of his need for someone to 'crowd [him] with love' and 'force [him] to care'. In both these last two sentences, notice the ambiguity that is still present in the verbs 'crowd' and 'force', as though it will take something dynamic and determined in order for him to change, despite his great desire for that change. Finally, the climax arrives with the three statements of the title words 'Being alive', each higher and more impassioned than the last. Here, being alive is characterized as being synonymous with being in a relationship.

Within this overall structure and narrative there are complex sentences containing unexpected words and juxtapositions that allow the performer to discover a detailed and individual interpretation of the song. Just take the first line and think about it for a moment. The usual sentiment in a love song is to want to be held 'close' and 'tight', often 'forever'. Here, there is the insertion of the word 'too' before 'close'. This completely changes the sentiment to reveal an awareness of the imperfections in relationships. The holding close may occur more or less often than one partner desires, and be more or less constricting than they require to feel safe. All this makes that little word 'too' of immense importance in imparting the need for something that is understood to be a compromise. It is a word that recurs throughout this song, and must be given due thought and attention.

The next line demands the hurts that come in any relationship. This is a different type of request from the previous one; the first was for closeness, but the second is for a sensation of pain. This pattern is followed in the second two phrases as Robert allows someone to sit in his chair, a relative inconvenience, and to ruin his sleep, which may be more profound (though not as profound as hurting him 'too deep'), but the reason for all this is stated next: that these indignities will make him aware that he is alive. So in singing these opening twelve bars, there are a myriad of possibilities for interpreting the individual words and phrases, bringing different colours and meanings to each that lead to the possibility that being alive (and being in a relationship with which it is paralleled) is actually painful and uncomfortable, but infinitely desirable.

The following twelve-bar section, which includes the phrase 'put me through hell and

Beverley Klein discovering her dilemma as she sings 'The crossword puzzle' by Maltby and Shire in Starting Here, Starting Now *(1997).*

The final part of the song contains similar ambiguities with a wish to be 'crowded' with love and 'forced' to care. But there is a strong commitment too, with 'I'll always be there as frightened as you, to help us survive being alive', which first of all makes the suggestion that being alive is something to be survived, but also notice that this is the first mention of the pronoun 'us'. Here at the climax of the song there is at last a sense of togetherness and its desirability to achieve a full experience of 'being alive'.

What I've tried to demonstrate in this close reading of the lyrics is the immense amount of detail contained in the song that can be drawn out of the interpretation of the words to add colour, so that each line is part of a whole but also substantially different. So if you are going to do the 'thought-changing' exercise during this song, you are likely to snap your fingers or raise your hand at the end, and even during the majority, of lines but, as with 'People will say we're in love', there is a larger narrative shape that represents a journey of discovery for the character.

On the Steps of the Palace

'On the steps of the palace' (number 13 in the vocal score, and there is also a DVD available of the Broadway production of *Into the Woods*) is the song Cinderella sings after leaving the ball on the third occasion. On the first and second evenings she has had a short exchange with the baker's wife after leaving the ball. On these occasions Cinderella sang and the baker's wife asked spoken questions about the prince. On the third evening when Cinderella runs from the palace she gets stuck on the staircase because the prince has anticipated her flight and 'spread pitch on the stairs'. The same musical material is developed in this song as

give me support for being alive' needs treating in a similar way, so that each word and each phrase is given due consideration and character. The middle of the song contains a series of rhythmically similar figures that build on the final words of the opening sections 'being alive'. Here again there is an ambiguity about how the character perceives what is on offer in a relationship with the words 'make me confused, mock me with praise, let me be used' before the perhaps much more positive 'vary my days'. The suggestion here is that being single, alone and in control can be too predictable. This is followed by the important statement that develops this sentiment: 'but alone is alone, not alive'.

was introduced in the earlier two scenes, Numbers 7 and 10C in the vocal score.

The song has an arch shape, beginning with the musical figure that had underscored the previous version of the song, but this time introduced more formally by the narrator; but it starts quite softly. In the earlier versions, the accompaniment begins and ends by being overlaid with dialogue as the characters continue their conversation and the song appears and disappears into its context. On this occasion, there is a formal beginning and ending to the song, marking it out, separating it and allowing for applause at the end, though it still has an arch shape. There is not a clear, single climax of the song, though the music gets busier and more harmonically and melodically complex, as Cinderella tries to decide what to do just before 'Better run along home'. The second place that might arguably be the climax is when she makes her decision 'Then from out of the blue, and without any guide, You know what your decision is', as this also marks a return of familiar melodic material.

The musical structure supports this reading of the song as having an arch shape, since similar musical material begins and ends the song and the intervening motifs also become familiar, though each is continually altered and developed. The A section runs from the start to the change of accompaniment at Bar 23. The B section runs to Bar 36 and is immediately followed by B1 (an extended version of the same musical material). C follows, running from Bar 57 until Bar 75, when the B section material returns. Bar 86 marks the next change to material identifiably developed from section A which leads back to A1. This makes the whole structure A B B1 C B2 A1.

THE SONG IN THE WHOLE WORK

We've looked at the process of making decisions to impart the sense of a journey through the song for the performer in the two examples above, so in this example I'm going to explore the place of character and performer in the performance situation.

- Who is the character singing to? Cinderella sings the song while standing alone, stuck on the steps of the palace having run from the ball. It is therefore a soliloquy revealing her gradual change of mind through her decision-making process. At the end of the song, she steps out of her shoe and runs home, leaving the shoe as a clue to her identity for the prince to find. She is therefore singing to the audience, though of course it is not present for the character, as she exists behind the fourth wall. But, more importantly, this is an overt revelation of her thought process so that the character can be more fully represented to the audience.

- What does she reveal? In the course of the song Cinderella reveals to the audience her own thought processes about the predicament she finds herself in and weighs the various options before making a decision. Through this process she also reveals how insecure she feels about the different status of herself and the prince. At the palace the relationship feels right, but she knows that she'll 'never belong', and that arriving at the ball is fun and exciting but also 'scary'. She questions whether she is, in fact, what a prince would want if he really knew her. These sentiments add depth to the understanding of the character and offer opportunities for revelation of vulnerability.

She refers to her home with her stepmother and stepsisters, and speaks of the fact that they don't care about her, but that life is easier there where she knows what to expect and where there is nothing to lose. The status quo is often easier to cope with than a dreamed of change.

- Why is the character singing? The character is singing in order to reveal the vulnerability she feels, and to share with the audience the decision-making process. In musical theatre the convention is that soliloquies and self-revelation happen in song. However, she is also singing because it provides a third repetition of a motif that was established the first time she left the ball. This pattern sets up the comic situation that the prince has put pitch on the stairs sticking her to the spot and allowing this moment of soliloquy, but it also provides a structural use of repetition of a theme with which the audience is now familiar. It is important as the climax of the ball, the development of this musical material, and the working out of this story, which leads very shortly to the Finale of Act One in which all the characters achieve a happy ending.

- What is the song saying? The song allows a perspective to be added to the story of Cinderella, which it is assumed everyone in the audience already knows. The audience is simultaneously aware of the usual narrative, perhaps through pantomime or fairy story, and this version of the plot, and notes the differences. It gives the prince and Cinderella different motivations in the working out of the plot than are normally presented, so you might consider that the prince traps Cinderella, who chooses a fatalistic response, not choosing but leaving a clue and seeing what happens. This situation, in contrast with the usual love story, allows the bleaker events of Act Two to follow.

In the analyses above I've tried to demonstrate that songs in musical theatre generally contain a journey for the character and a revelation of emotional vulnerability. It is unlikely that characters would be able to reveal these vulnerabilities in speech, but song offers that opportunity when, supported by appropriate music, they find themselves able to open their hearts. The task for the performer, therefore, is to discover the details of the song, but also have a sense of the journey the character must undertake to fulfil their function in the story, and a sense of how the song contributes to the structure of the whole work.

10 ROCK AND POP SONGS

The reason the genre of rock musicals needs separate consideration is that the style of singing needs to change to reflect the musical style. A different vocal quality is required that is appropriate to the music (and its increased volume) and the character. This is characterized by a lower vocal range for women, and often a higher vocal range for men (think about the ranges of Jesus and Mary in *Jesus Christ Superstar* or Ché and Evita in *Evita*), and a full-throated belt that is rougher and has a less controlled sound than that used in the musicals discussed so far. Equally, there is greater use of a quiet, breathy quality, especially for intimate or tender emotional moments, and the opportunity to use catches and sobs or broken sounds, again to represent deep emotion. There is a desire for a certain roughness of quality and production to represent the authenticity of the working person, the person of the streets that is characterized by a vocal technique that sounds rougher, less controlled, and less practised. These vocal techniques all need practice, however, because they can easily damage the voice if not used carefully. In some cases, it simply wouldn't be possible to recreate the sounds for weeks or months of performances without a technical strategy to protect the voice while producing a semblance of the 'rock' sound.

There are other characteristics of rock-musical performance too, such as the much greater use of the glottal onset, an individual approach to the use of ornamentation as part of the interpretation of a song, freedom to adapt the rhythm in the same way to reflect the interpretation of the song and character, rhythmic freedom to lean against the beat so that the articulation of a word occurs before or after the beat, shorter phrases and more breaks for breath, and less vibrato. The deviation from the melody and rhythm as written is a significant difference between singing rock musicals and other musicals, as it draws on the traditions of rock music, which is historically a predominantly oral genre. So, the singer often has a much greater leeway in developing their own musical interpretation of character and situation within these musicals than in other types of musical theatre. However, there is one absolute difference between singing pop or rock songs in a pop or rock concert and singing similar songs in a musical-theatre performance. There is a tendency for pop and rock performers to close their eyes and emote for themselves rather than revealing the emotional vulnerability of the character for the audience. In musical theatre, you must allow the audience to share in the emotion, and therefore you should avoid singing with your eyes closed.

LEARNING A ROCK SONG

Characteristics of a Rock Sound

- Lower vocal range for women, higher vocal range for men.
- Use of breathy and broken sounds.
- Less vibrato.
- Increased use of glottal stop or glottal onset.
- The use of slides up or down at the end of a phrase.
- Greater freedom to ornament the melody and alter the rhythm.
- A rough or aggressive tone and a highly emotional delivery.
- The use of belt sounds or forward placing to produce full-throated and emotional climaxes characteristic of rock and pop music.
- Sometimes less importance is placed on the words, but emphasis on the sound itself and the melodic ornamentation to express emotion.

When learning a song from a rock musical, for the first time in this book I will say, listen to all the recordings that are available of the song. This is because the notation of rock music is often simplified, and because, as I said above, there is room for musical interpretation to represent the character. In songs from other parts of the repertoire, for the most part, ornamentation is not appropriate and sometimes would be detrimental, since the music is written out in a more detailed way, but if, for example, you look at the score of *The Rocky Horror Show* you will discover that if you sing what is written, it will sound very stilted and has little resemblance to the sounds you might hear on a recording or the way you might interpret the character. However, note that I say to listen to all the recordings that are available. This is

because you don't want to copy someone else's interpretation but to get a feel for the song and the character so that you can develop your own interpretation, which is likely to include some variations of rhythm and melodic ornamentation. As examples in this section I'm going to begin by looking at some of the songs from *The Rocky Horror Show*, but rather than going into depth about each song as I have in previous chapters, I'm going to offer ways of thinking about individual moments, which each raise different issues.

SLIDES, GLOTTALS AND SOBS

Touch a Touch Me

To begin with, let's consider the first lines of Janet's song 'Touch a touch me'. Although the lines into the song (Columbia and Magenta saying 'Tell us about it, Janet' and laughing) are a very clear cue for a song in a cod musical-theatre way, Janet needs to remember that she is both performer and character, and to respond both to the comedy of the 'cue for a song' moment and the need for the character to be vulnerable in exposing her history and emotions. In a rock musical that means that she might begin the song with a breathy sound and some hesitation in the rhythm developed from an acting approach to the words. But there's more. The very first line 'I was feeling done in' could begin either with a breathy, slightly pathetic anticipation to the word 'I', which would now be pronounced 'hhah'. This approach might also be pitched slightly below the note so that there is a swoop up to the first word, but the arrival on the note needs to be timed with the arrival on the vowel. The sound might also be slightly nasal to represent her self-pity. Playing this moment as slightly

Richard O'Brien listening to the band rehearse for the European tour of **The Rocky Horror Show** *(1991).*

pathetic is likely to lead to a slower delivery of the words and a longer sustained note at the end of the phrase, and therefore vibrato on the final word of the phrase 'in'.

Alternatively, there can be more of a plaintive quality, the sound of someone about to cry, accentuated with a glottal attack on the word 'I', which is likely to be followed by a shorter note on the word 'in' and so no opportunity for vibrato. Or you could try any combination of these features to achieve the emotional effect you want. In any case, there is no way that the rhythm should have the regu-

larity of the printed music; it should be sung in short phrases, following the groupings in the score, but with the actual rhythmic patterns adapted to those of the speech of the character.

The second feature I want to draw attention to in this opening verse is that higher notes, which in other parts of musical-theatre singing might be 'covered' so that they don't stick out of the melodic line, tend to be accentuated in this style of singing. So, in the phrase 'it only leads to trouble.... And seat wetting', the two raised notes 'leads' and 'And' can be accentuated. They are also likely to have slides up to them, especially the 'And' on which you can experiment with glottal attacks, slides, vibrato or even a 'sob' on the beginning of the word. Each of these would be part of a different interpretation of what the character is saying in this admission – presumably she is intimating that this is an experience she has had, but how does she feel about that experience? That colour needs to be created not through the words alone, but by the sound of the voice as Janet sings those words.

Once in a While

The following song in the show is Brad singing 'Once in a while' in a cod country-and-western style. Here you might consider some of the characteristics of that style. In particular, when the same vowel sound is sung over several notes you would normally sing the line smoothly in musical theatre, but in country rock you might re-articulate each note. So, for example, instead of singing 'she don't want to call you', you might sing 'ca-ha-ha-hall you' with a broken sound on the breath, requiring a little bounce of the diaphragm for each 'ha', which might represent little sobs. These are not the sobs of someone actually crying, but a device of this type of music that you can choose to use or not, but having the backing singers allows this sort of exaggeration in the musical line. It is likely, too, that you will slide up to many notes, especially those beginning with a vowel. So whereas the intention in singing the word 'once' in most musicals would be to explode the vowel 'w' and arrive cleanly on the vowel as quickly as possible, in this style it is very different. The note is likely to begin at least a tone lower than the written score suggests on a rising 'www', so that the 'ah' sound and the opening of the lips that

Don Gallagher as Brad in the Farnham Repertory Theatre production of Rocky Horror Show *(1985).*

begins the word 'once' occurs at the moment of arrival on the correct pitch, thus extending the use of the consonant, the slide and the rather nasal, whining sound it creates.

In the next line there is the potential for further distortion of vowel sounds in the phrase 'speaking on the telephone'. Instead of a smooth unbroken progression between the words, in this style one might introduce a glottal stop and slide before the word 'on'. The phrase then contains a tiny break after the word 'speaking' to close the vocal folds to articulate the hard attack to the vowel 'o', which might be distorted with a slight southern twang. This is followed by the opportunity for another 'sob' sound on 'pho-hone'.

In this song, you can also experiment with the length of phrases. The written score contains very short phrases with opportunities to breathe after every few words. In many musical-theatre songs you would expect to sing through some of these phrases, especially as you build towards a climax to represent increasing passion. Here, though, passion can be represented in that way, or it can be represented by the broken phrases, glottal attacks and 'sob' sounds that are implied in the melodic line. Depending on how the character is being played, you would choose to include more or less of these effects. The more you include the more comical and caricatured the delivery will appear, the fewer you include, and the closer the delivery is to that of most types of musical-theatre singing, the more 'realistic' and sympathetic Brad will appear. However, the artistry of the delivery will need to include all of these features in some combination so that the wit of the style and genre are present, while not detracting from the opportunity for audiences to empathize with Brad's plight.

CREATING A 'BELT' SOUND

The other distinctive feature of a rock sound is the ability to 'belt', or make a sound that is open and full-throated that may be akin to a controlled and pitched shout. There are, of course, examples of this in *The Rocky Horror Show*, but I'm going to look at two songs from *Little Shop of Horrors*, which require this sort of delivery. 'Suddenly Seymour' is sung by both Seymour and Audrey, while the song for the plant, Audrey II, 'Feed me' also contains Seymour's high rock section 'I don't know'. Both of these songs also have the potential for adding some ornamentation, but that is even more fully exemplified in the examples below

from *Dreamgirls* that require an even more extensive 'belt' sound and a great inventiveness in ornamentation.

'Suddenly Seymour' begins with the breathy quality and short phrases described above. Seymour dares to speak to Audrey of his feelings for her, as he protects and saves her. The change of quality to a full-throated 'belt' may occur during the phrase 'but now they're okay' so that the crescendo is triggered by the sentiment of that phrase. Equally, Seymour (and the musical director) might choose a sudden change of volume and sound colour on the word 'Suddenly'. At the end of the chorus Audrey sings a verse and chorus, beginning with a breathy quality and speech-based rhythmic patterns for the explanation of the verse, before breaking into a full-throated celebration at the start of the chorus, also on the word 'Suddenly'. The lines of the third verse are split between the two characters before the final chorus is sung, mostly in unison, building to an impassioned and climactic finish.

The essential difference between singing with the technique used for songs of the classic era of the musical and using pop and belt sounds is in the mix of sound qualities and how the notes are approached. For the classic musicals you will generally have a controlled and 'covered' sound. To discover this sound, sing 'miaow' on a falling phrase and feel how the sound feels centred in the head and face. To give weight to lower notes you can add a little of the chest quality. Practise this by sliding down an octave and finishing on a note in your chest register. Don't push down on the final note, but find the sensation that the note is being sung from the controlled position above, but with extra vibration from expanding into the chest quality.

When singing in pop and rock songs you

111

Creating a Belt Sound

- Create space in the back of the throat by raising the soft palate (the feeling of being about to yawn).
- Extend the space even further by feeling that you are about to smile in the muscles at the back of the throat.
- Think that your whole neck is expanding to create as much room as possible.
- Keep your tongue forward with the tip behind the lower teeth and the middle of the tongue reaching the side of the upper teeth (as though about to sing a very open 'ee' sound).
- Anchor the feet firmly on the ground – feel as though you are rooting yourself like a tree into the ground.
- Breathe in and then use the muscles of the diaphragm and torso to project the air through the barrel-like open space of the upper body, throat and mouth.
- Begin by creating a squeaking sound like a seagull to check that you have sufficient openness before practising bigger sounds.
- Begin by practising these big sounds in the middle of your range, sliding up and down as in the exercises in earlier chapters – don't attempt everything at once but build your range gradually.
- If you feel the slightest tickle or blockage stop, relax your whole body, check for tension, especially in your jaw and throat, release it and then begin carefully to set yourself up again.
- Make sure that you are creating vibrations in the mask of the face, as well as the neck and chest – many people feel that the cheekbones or the centre of the forehead are the focal points for singing higher notes with this quality of sound.

will generally find that the mix is more weighted and controlled from the lower registers, but if you push down too hard you will create a break in your voice and won't be able to access the upper register. Therefore, to achieve the belt sound, or even simply to add volume and emotion in this style of singing, you need to achieve a large, open space in the mouth and throat, with the tongue resting forward so that it doesn't interfere with the positioning of the vocal cords or cause tension in the throat. Strong support from the muscles of the torso is required to send the air up onto the resonator of the hard palate. However, this sound is not made only in the chest region or used in the lower register. The belt is also a mix of sounds using the mask of the face to add vibration and carrying power, while the roughness and openness of the body give the sense of an authentic and emotional quality.

Prepare yourself, as described in the instructions above and, when you are ready, sing the first phrase of the chorus on a very open 'ee' sound. Experiment with the tone and where you can feel vibrations. Sing through the chorus, still using only 'ee', as this will encourage you to engage the mask of the face. Slide all the intervals, especially the rising ones so that you experiment with the vocal colour on the high notes matching it to the lower colour. However, it is really important that you stop and check for tension in your body and especially in your face and jaw, as many people create this sound by tightening the jaw. Check repeatedly that your jaw is mobile as you sing through this phrase. You should not need much breath to sing in this way, so if you feel that you are running out of breath quickly you are probably not providing sufficient support in the lower body or sufficient focus in the sound. Listen and make sure you are creating a clean, not a breathy sound. Later, when you are completely confident with your ability to use this sound quality you will be able to explore, introducing cracks and breaks in the sound as special effects. As with all the exercises in the first half of this book, putting the words in will tend to encourage you to close down some parts of the mechanism, so work through each phrase making sure that you re-open the throat and raise the soft palate fully for each vowel.

Looking back at the refrain of 'Suddenly Seymour', you will discover that the highest note is just over an octave above middle C. That is perfectly fine within this style of singing, as long as you create a mixed sound incorporating the focus on the mask of the face with the chest quality. However, you will not be able to sing this note if your body, jaw or tongue is tight, or if you are pushing the sound down into your chest. You need to feel that the sound is being fired from the body, but is vibrating in the face and being sent out and expanding into a large space. Without this sense of outward projection or the mix of sounds you could damage your voice, so be careful, and, as with all the exercises in the first half of the book, build your voice gradually.

ORNAMENTATION IN ROCK SONGS

The second song from *Little Shop of Horrors* that I want to consider briefly is 'Feed me'. This

Drums, electronic instruments and amplification required for rock musicals: The Rocky Horror Show *band for the European tour (1986–87).*

song is an excellent example of the impossibility of accurately notating what a singer might actually sing in this style. Various singers of this part have introduced different ornamentations, shouts, cries and even the use of falsetto voice. In particular, perhaps you might focus on the section beginning 'Would you like a cadillac car?'. It is set very high in the range, but it needs excellent articulation and therefore forward placing so that the words are understood. This means that you can't use a full-throated belt sound as you can't articulate quickly or clearly enough for this phrase, but you need the openness and the support of the belt sound to create the sound quality required. One of the tricks in this sort of phrase, apart from listening to many versions and copying each of them to discover how other people have approached the ornamentation and colouring of this phrase, is to approach it almost as talk-singing in an almost shouted pitch, with swoops and slides after the notes. Whereas in the earlier songs we looked at sliding into a note from below, here, you can explore sliding up and off a note creating the sensation of rising from the note rather than falling off it.

Seymour's response is even higher and contains long phrases that are regularly ornamented by the singer. This section needs the openness of the belt technique, but also needs the playfulness with sound that was introduced in discussing 'Once in a while' in the *Rocky Horror Show*, though without the repeated articulations of sustained notes, which are specific to the country and western style. Here, you might explore the use of nasal sounds, whines and sighs during the sustained notes.

One more song for male voices that you might want to explore, if you have good control of the higher range of your voice, is 'Gethsemane' from *Jesus Christ Superstar*. It contains examples of all the features addressed in this chapter including the breathiness at the start, the fast articulation at high pitch, the ornamentation and the extension of the voice with sobs, shouts and cries.

To develop your skills in ornamentation and playing with colour further you could explore the songs from the musical *Dreamgirls*. These are extremely difficult songs that require immense vocal control, so I suggest them only when you feel confident of your technique, but also, think of them as exercises that you explore parts of, rather than as complete, songs to sing. The most well-known is 'For one night only', which requires fast articulation and placing on the mask of the face to create a strong pop sound. A slower lyrical song is 'Family', and a complete *tour de force* that you should listen to, but perhaps not attempt yet, is 'And I am telling you I'm not going'. This, like 'Gethsemane' in the male repertoire is to be admired, learned from and aspired to at this stage.

However, although I've introduced you to some very difficult material to listen to, the requirements are the same, and you can apply these techniques to many other popular songs, such as the songs from *Grease*, which are much easier, have a much smaller range, and are great fun.

11 COMEDY AND PATTER SONGS

Comedy, character and patter songs come in many shapes and sizes. The common features from a singer's perspective are that they require a smaller vocal range (in many cases), clear articulation and some variation of 'speak-singing' to interpret the extremity of the verbal ingenuity. While maintaining the character, the performer must also be aware of genre, irony and pastiche, so that the audience's attention is drawn to the comedy through the characterization. However, these songs are fun to sing because they offer the opportunity for extreme characterizations and outrageous sentiments. I will break this enormous range of songs into three groups: patter and point songs revolving around witty word-play and gags; extreme sentiments by larger-than-life characters, entitled 'character songs'; pastiche and satire, which may also be used in the other groups, but requires some separate consideration.

PATTER AND POINT SONGS

The most well-known patter songs are contained in the works of Gilbert and Sullivan, made popular in Britain and America in the late-nineteenth century and still performed by amateurs and professionals. The majority of performances of these operettas are new productions of the material, such as Jonathan Miller's production of *The Mikado* at the English National Opera in 1986, but there have also been significant adaptations of either book or musical style. *The Hot Mikado* (1939) was later followed by *Hot Mikado* (1986) by David Bell and Rob Bowman. *Pirates of Penzance* was updated by Joseph Papp (1980), and a new narration written by Ian Hislop accompanied a performance of *Iolanthe* at the Proms in 2000. These all provide patter

Henry Lytton as the Major General in The Pirates of Penzance *in the 1920s.*

songs (for men) that are widely known, such as 'I am the very model of a modern major-general' from *The Pirates of Penzance*, 'I've got a little list' from *The Mikado* or the nightmare song from *Iolanthe*.

Patter songs became a feature of music-hall in Britain, but were also an influence for subsequent musical-theatre composers in songs that might more correctly be regarded as point songs. These are songs in which verbal gags predominate. Patter songs also contain verbal gags but are strongly characterized by the apparently excessive speed of delivery and the dexterity required to articulate the words. In Britain, think, for example, of Noel Coward's 'Has anybody seen our ship?' or 'The passenger's always right', which are closer to patter songs, or, in the United States, of Cole Porter's 'You're the top' or 'Friendship' or Dietz and Schwartz's 'That's entertainment', or even Sondheim and Styne's 'You gotta have a gimmick' from *Gypsy*, which might all be regarded as point songs, though they contain the influence of patter songs. More recently the influence of patter songs is felt in comedy songs such as 'The elements' by Tom Lehrer set to the music of Arthur Sullivan's 'I am the very model of a modern major-general' (from *An Evening Wasted with Tom Lehrer*).

Both these types of lyric-writing lend themselves to songs that interrupt the events of the plot for the joy of indulging in excessive and exaggerated word-play. They are less evident in contemporary musicals, though the word-play is still apparent used in the service of particular characters, as, for example, in Stephen Sondheim's 'And another hundred people' from *Company*, or 'Buddy's blues' from *Follies* or in Richard Maltby and David Shire's 'Crossword puzzle' from the revue *Starting Here, Starting Now*.

Characteristics of Patter and Point Songs

Patter songs:
- verbal dexterity in articulation;
- clear but repetitive and excessive narrative;
- fast-paced performance;
- alliteration and clear rhyme patterns to challenge expectations of multiple rhymes;
- regular and repetitive verbal rhythms;
- excessive use of long, archaic or unusual words to make unusual rhymes;
- limited melodic range and rhythmic variety;
- focus on the performance of the song as much as the content;
- often use a form of speak-singing.

Point songs:
- a series of verbal gags lead through a narrative to the final punch line at the end;
- less focus on pace than clever word-play and witticisms;
- multiple rhymes, alliteration and internal rhymes;
- limited melodic range;
- repeated choruses and motifs;
- use of popular music styles;
- often use a form of speak-singing.

I am the Very Model of a Modern Major General

The performer of the Gilbert and Sullivan song 'I am the very model of a modern major-general' is telling two stories simultaneously to the audience. The first story is that being outlined in the words of the song, which in this case is the recounting of the many facts and strategies that the major-general knows, so depicting the character of the major-general.

The second story is the one that the performer is sharing with the audience about the difficulty of singing the song and managing to breathe.

The first task when learning this song is, therefore, to work out the sentence structure and phrasing, and the breathing of each section. For example, instead of breathing at the end of each line, one might choose to phrase 'and I quote the fights historical, from Marathon to Waterloo, in order categorical;' as one sentence, though phrased with the punctuation to clarify the meaning of the line and highlight the rhyme. At the same time, the musical rhythm is constant, so that the breathing places are minute and the breath must be snatched. For the most part this must be worked into the delivery, but there are places in the song where the pace can alter to follow that of the performer, giving space for comedy business. There is often a slight holding back at the end of the first-half of the verse to allow for this, and in fact there is a pause bar written into the score to allow for business here, while the second-half of each verse maintains a strict tempo so that the repeated lines sung by the chorus can mimic the delivery by the soloist. The final verse ('in fact when I know what is meant by "mamelon" and "ravelin",') is marked 'slower' in the score with a final pause after 'elemental strategy' before the lively vivace of the lines 'You'll say a better major-general has never sat a gee' through to the end.

This playing with the pace of delivery to allow for interaction with the audience and the other performers, and the pausing for comedy business, is a feature of these types of songs of this period, but only at certain moments. To indulgently pull the pace faster or slower throughout the song defeats the object, which is the demonstration of articulatory dexterity, and the comedy of the performer's ability to remember the words and find moments to breathe. This demonstration of the ability to sing tongue-twisters is reproduced in later patter songs that derive from this model, such as 'Moses supposes' in *Singin' in the Rain*, but since this song, like 'Be a clown' or 'That's entertainment' in the film of that name, is filmed, the audience interaction is not present and so the song only contains the wit of the lyric, and therefore the musical tempo is rather more consistent throughout the song.

The second characteristic of the patter song is the use of a style of 'speak-singing' in which the singer moves fluidly between sung notes and notes that are spoken at approximately the musical pitch. In order to make this transposition between speech and song without a change of vocal quality, the sung delivery needs to be placed forward in the mouth and use the resonances of the mask of the face. There is no time for the rounder, mellower sounds of the chest register, but the clarity and carrying power of the vibrations of the facial cavities are activated along with the dynamic articulation of words by the active use of lips, tongue and teeth. The tongue-twister exercises given in Chapter 3 are the key to the delivery of patter and point songs. There are sections of songs that can be more lyrical – that are more sung – while other parts of the song are not sustained, but even the lyrical sections rely on a forward placing and clear articulation. There are examples of this in the duet 'Friendship' by Cole Porter from *DuBarry was a Lady* and used in *Anything Goes*.

Friendship
The degree to which the delivery deviates from the musical score varies according to the

performer and the performance, but the musical shape and the rhythm of the phrase must be discernible, so that the melodic and rhythmic character of the song is retained. So, for example, the first two lines could be half-spoken in rhythm or completely sung depending on the characterization, but by the time you arrive at the third line 'If you ever feel so happy you land in jail, I'm your bail' the pitch of the phrase and the extension of the sentence through two lines means that this is likely to be sung. The refrain, 'It's friendship...dig, dig, dig' must be sung, especially since the melody is usually performed by the two characters in harmony. Finding the right balance of speech and song is a process of trial and error, but it is imperative to know the melody thoroughly

before deviating from it, otherwise you will not be able to hook into and out of the melody, and you will not speak-sing in the melodic and rhythmic patterns that characterize the song.

Brush up your Shakespeare

A rather slower song that might be considered a point song rather than a patter song, but which certainly derives from a music-hall tradition and which relies on speak-singing for clear articulation of the witty lyrics, is 'Brush up your Shakespeare' also by Cole Porter from *Kiss me Kate*. In this song, the comedy is not only that the two gangsters are doing a successful music-hall routine, but that they devise outrageous rhymes to incorporate the titles of many of Shakespeare's plays. Here the

Mary Lincoln speak-singing Noel Coward's 'Has anybody seen our ship?' in **Has Anybody Seen my Tiddler?** *Falmouth Arts Centre (1998).*

performer needs to articulate the rhymes so that the punch-lines of the gags (the points) are clear. The line 'the wife of the British Embessida' requires an over-the-top English accent to set up the rhyme with 'Troilus and Cressida'. More complicated is 'If she says your behaviour is heinous', which sets up the rhyme for the punch-line 'kick her right in the Coriolanus'. Here two gags are simultaneously presented – the finding of the rhyme for 'heinous' and the hidden pun highlighted in the second half of the word 'Coriolanus'.

The common feature of all these songs is that the words contain the witticisms and gags and the music serves it. However, that doesn't mean that the music is unimportant; it must be used effectively to highlight the comic potential of the words through the use of judicious tempo variation and, more often, constancy of pace, deviation between speech and song, direct delivery to an audience and potentially audience interaction, if appropriate. Moreover, although these songs all have a place in a musical, they do not always develop the plot but are often moments of artifice and enjoyment, when the audience simply enjoys the verbal ingenuity rather than expecting character or plot development, so sing and enjoy them for their own sake.

CHARACTER SONGS

Crossword Puzzle
The next group of songs are those that require

Kristin Blaikie singing 'I'm going to make you beautiful' from **Starting Here, Starting Now,** *Maltby and Shire, Exeter (1997).*

or rely on extreme characterizations, and there are a huge number of these that performers enjoy performing. 'Crossword puzzle' by Richard Maltby Jr and David Shire is both a character song and a patter song because it combines the use of verbal ingenuity with the gradual revelation of information about the character and the situation. One of the most effective aspects of this lyric is the double use of words as the character flips between telling the story of her relationship with Hecky and doing the crossword. So, for example, the line 'the answer would leap in my' is interrupted by the reading of the word 'Hartebeest' to which the answer in the crossword is 'Gnu'. But the pun of 'heart' and 'harte' provides a link between the two stories. In fact all the clues in the crossword can be related to the broken relationship, alongside the gradual revelation, by the character to herself and the audience, that maybe her competitive streak had been to some extent responsible for the break-up. She realizes that 'perhaps that's why I'm left here on the shelf; Perhaps he wanted to get the long ones by himself'. Finally, she also discovers that loudly demonstrated quickness of brain and competitive intelligence are not adequate substitutes for common sense and sensitivity, as she sings 'If I weren't so dumb, I'd be spending this Sunday in a church hearing wedding chimes'. So this song uses the tools of patter and point songs: the fast pace, the clever wordplay, the forward placing and clear articulation; but adds to it the development of character and the gradual revelation of a situation.

There are many other songs in the revue *Starting Here, Starting Now* that fall into this category, but I will refer you to only two, as they are available in the vocal selection. The first is 'I don't remember Christmas' sung by a man in the revue but is sung by men or women in auditions. It is set at the end of an affair as the singer tries to forget – or at least to convince himself that he has forgotten – the lost lover 'I don't remember crying, and I can't recall your touch, 'Cause I'd never be so stupid as to open up so much'. Throughout the song, of course, it is apparent that he thinks of her all the time. The second song is 'I think I may want to remember today' that recounts a woman's rediscovery of someone she knew many years ago who has grown up in a way that pleases her; 'my how you've grown'. These are both well worth looking at and learning as they're fun, relatively modern and allow for the development of interesting characters.

Adelaide's Lament

One of the most important things to think about when preparing these character songs is creating the voice for the character. The well-known example is the squeaky voice of Adelaide in *Guys and Dolls*, but what you have to weigh up against creating an outrageous voice is how often you are going to have to perform the song, how long the run of the show is and whether it might potentially cause damage to your voice. However, you could, for example, use a more nasal sound than you might normally use, both because of Adelaide's cold and in order to make the voice more grating than a heroine's voice might sound. Then you might play with the accent and characterization, exploring the legacy of 'dumb blonde' characters typified by Marilyn Monroe in *Some Like it Hot*. However, Adelaide has to secure and retain the audience's sympathy, so although you can introduce these comic features into the vocal colour and accent, and it's clearly there in the words, you

Some More Character Songs

There are much more extreme characterizations in songs from throughout musical-theatre history. The ones for women seem to be more frequent and more extreme. They include:

- 'I cain't say no' from *Oklahoma*;
- 'Adelaide's lament' from *Guys and Dolls*;
- 'Just you wait' from *My Fair Lady*;
- 'Somewhere that's green' from *Little Shop of Horrors*;
- 'You can always count on me' from *City of Angels*.

There are a large number of character songs for women in the musicals of Stephen Sondheim, including:

- 'Broadway baby';
- 'The ladies who lunch';
- 'I will marry the miller's son';
- 'Leave you';
- 'I'm still here'.

However, there are also extreme characterizations for men, including:

- 'The "god-why-don't-you-love-me" blues' from *Follies* (also known as 'Buddy's blues'), a music-hall patter song in which Buddy has a nervous breakdown;
- 'King Herod's song' from *Jesus Christ Superstar*, a parody of a music-hall song and dance number;
- you may not regard the MC's songs from *Cabaret*, 'Two ladies' and 'The gorilla song' as quite in this category, but they also call for an extreme characterization and certainly have a point to make;
- 'The dentist's song' from *Little Shop of Horrors*, which I will discuss below.

have to allow Adelaide's vulnerability to be present and credible too. Look for moments to demonstrate vulnerability, such as 'she's getting a kind of a name for herself and the name ain't "his"', or 'when they get on the train for Niag'ra and she can hear church bells chime'. Such moments allow the audience to share the sadness and despair that highlight and give meaning to the comedy of the sneezing, wheezing and coughing, the nasal sound and the grotesque accent.

The Dentist

The dentist in *Little Shop of Horrors* is set up through the first-half of the show as a sadistic bully who is beating up the heroine. The song itself is usually performed as a kind of Elvis impersonation to highlight the machismo and self-love of the character, and you can have great fun with the vocal and physical gestures. But somehow, the words have to be heard and the character also has to be played for real; the clue here is his relationship with his mother. The dentist is telling the audience a story about his relationship with his mother, so although the gag lines, and particularly the first mention of his chosen career that will 'make your natural tendencies pay', must be sung with gusto and clarity and awareness of the comedy, the whole song is told from the perspective of a boy who loves his dead mother.

The idea of a dentist having chosen that career because he loves causing pain is black comedy and provides a sense of the grotesque, but keep in mind the vision that he is doing this to make his mother proud, and you have another layer of reasoning behind this character, and a way of finding a grotesque justification for his self-love and arrogance. This, then, can be played to excess. Finding these ways into a character can give you ways to present them so that the audience has complex feelings about them rather than simply reproducing a stereotypical evil villain (although that is also fun) or a perfect hero. These character songs contain these possibilities for finding moments of vulnerability and complexity alongside the comedy that allow the audience to laugh and cry, to identify with the character and to recognize the grotesque caricature.

PASTICHE AND SATIRE

The final group of songs I want to introduce to you here use satire or pastiche. *Oh What a Lovely War!* uses a pastiche of the style of a pierrot show, to highlight the difference of mood between the comic songs, dances and routines, and the facts and events being portrayed in the wartime narrative. The contrast needs to be highlighted, so the pierrot-show moments have to be performed with light-hearted glee and over-the-top high spirits. The effect of this combination is a satirical commentary on the wartime events. A pastiche uses a combination of well-known references, or in this case musical styles. The reason for creating a pastiche can be ironic or satirical but it can also simply be used for comic effect.

John Kander and Fred Ebb use pastiche in creating the glamour and glitz of the 1930s in 'Razzle dazzle' to satirize the credibility of the legal system in the courtroom scene in *Chicago*. The musical style or genre combines with what is being presented physically and verbally to produce a caricature. Frank 'n' Furter in *The Rocky Horror Show* sings 'Sweet transvestite' in a rock style that signifies a stereotype of posing male sexuality (though I'm not sure this could be regarded as satiri-

> ### Pastiche and Satire
>
> A pastiche can be a collection of new and known works put together to form a new combination. It can also be an imitation of another style, which can be used for comic or other effects – it is in this sense I use it here.
>
> The object of satire is to make fun of something (often people in power or institutions) in order to bring about change through the criticism. It can be accomplished by grotesque imitation, sarcasm, irony, parody or pastiche.

cal). The version of 'Like a virgin' in the film *Moulin Rouge* contrasts references to Madonna's video of the song with the outrageous caricature of the leader of the acting troupe singing the song in drag. This performance is used for comic effect but is also part of a black comedy. A different effect is created by the use of the song 'Roxanne' with a tango performance, which often signifies excessive or rampant sexuality, intercut with the rape of the heroine. The tango is used again in *Chicago* in 'The Cell Block Tango' to demonstrate the passion of the murderesses and satirize the judicial system that they are manipulating.

Although the use of well-known songs for comic effect is common in British pantomime, in musicals it is usually the musical styles that carry particular connotations. I mentioned the use of tango to signify a hot, Latin passion, which is utilized to great effect in *Evita*, and especially in the new London production directed by Michael Grandage with choreography (drawing heavily on tango) by Rob Ashford. A much more comic use of tango can be found in Tom Lehrer's 'Masochism tango'.

Set of **Cabaret** *at Harrogate Theatre (1988).*

The agony of sado-masochistic sex is linked to the passion of tango signified through the music to produce a highly grotesque comic caricature. In fact, many of Tom Lehrer's songs rely on the use of well-known musical styles, which are then juxtaposed with the lyrics. A pleasant waltz, usually used for words of love, is undermined by the knowledge that love will die 'when you're old and getting fat', and nationalist pride is undermined in the style and referring to the lyrics of southern American folk songs in 'I wanna go back to Dixie' whose lyric includes the line 'I wanna talk with southern gentlemen And put my white sheet on again, I ain't seen one good lynch-in' in years'. In these songs the style of the songs allows the singer to sing in the voice of the stereotype s/he is critiquing.

A very different effect is created, also using pastiche, in *Cabaret* when Herr Schultz's passion for Fraulein Schneider is expressed by the gift of a pineapple to the romantic lilt of a Hawaiian guitar in 'It couldn't please me more'. Their ill-fated love has this delightful comic moment, played completely straight by the performers, in which their love is expressed through the unexpected gift that they will keep 'not to eat, but see'. Another type of heroic male is created in *Into the Woods* in which the princes sing of their heroic quest for the female love object who is 'the only thing out of your reach' using a rhythm and melody reminiscent of 'The impossible dream' from *Man of la Mancha*. Again, what we see on the stage is a stereotype of the handsome heroic male of fairy-tale who is 'everything maidens could wish for'. Here the musical reference is to the impossible, and therefore unfulfilled, quest

123

that turns out to be what the princes really desire, as they ask 'what's as intriguing... as what's out of reach'. In terms of performance, the vocal style has to reflect the heroic stereotype, but to be expressed in an excessive way so that the audience is aware of the pastiche, and thus of the weakness and foolishness of the princes.

The vocal qualities of all these styles varies as the vocal quality needs to be appropriate to the musical genre. So the heroic princes need to capture the tone of 1930s heroic tenors, but play with the excesses of that genre, while Audrey in *Little Shop of Horrors* is another dumb blonde, possibly with a lisp and an exaggerated New York accent, though, as we saw in the previous chapter, she has her moments of love and tragedy when her vocal quality befits that state. Tango singers might need to capture something of the hoarseness and roughness of Argentinian street singers, alongside the rhythmic attack that caricatures the genre. Each interpretation will vary depending on the character, the production and the musical style, but awareness of genre and understanding of comic caricature offers the performer the opportunity to have fun with these songs.

What is common to all these comic styles is an understanding by the performer of the stereotypes and genres that are being used to create a comic caricature but, at the same time, a conviction by the character that allows vulnerability and weakness to be revealed, and empathy, irony or satire to be provided for the audience. The singer needs to create a heightened or larger-than-life character that is played for real, but in the awareness of the stereotypes they are using. This then reflexively focuses the audience's attention on the ironic, satirical, parodic or simply comic effects that are being produced.

12 AUDITIONING AND PERFORMING

So now the day has arrived when you feel confident enough to consider going for an audition. This might be for an amateur musical-theatre show or pantomime, or for a professional show, or season (as in repertory theatre or at, for example, a holiday camp or on a cruise ship). In either case, the most important piece of advice I can give you is to be well-prepared. Find out in advance who you will be meeting, the show or job that is being auditioned for, the part for which you are being considered, what material the panel wants to hear, whether there will be an accompanist (at most professional auditions there will be) and the time, date and venue of the audition and for the performances. It is important that you don't waste the panel's time going to auditions for jobs you couldn't do.

I will return to the issue of preparing material, but first let us consider the audition venue. It may be a theatre, in which case it is likely that you and the accompanist will be onstage and the panel in the auditorium. This can be a cold experience, but it gives you the opportunity to demonstrate how confident you are in the larger space, how you can command the space and how your performance will fill the whole auditorium. In this scenario you will have less opportunity to have a conversation with the panel, but will need to be

prepared to perform immediately and leave when finished. In the UK, in all but the largest casting sessions, the audition is more likely to be held in a rehearsal space in which you and the panel share the space. This is often easier to deal with as you can see and speak to the panel before performing, and you are likely to be invited to sit and speak with the panel either before or after you perform your pieces. In any case, if you audition regularly you will get to know the rehearsal and audition spaces and begin to feel more at home. You will know where (or indeed whether) there is a space nearby for you to warm up your voice, how to get there, and whether there is somewhere comfortable to sit while you wait or to change clothes, if necessary.

The second thought I want to share with you, before getting down to the nitty gritty of preparing and performing at an audition, is that the panel has a show that it wants to cast. The panel members and any support staff who might read with you, accompany you or simply tick your name off when you arrive, want everyone who walks through the door to do well and to be perfect for the roles they are looking to fill. They have no interest in being difficult or off-putting, they will generally do all they can to help you feel at ease within the constraints of what is usually a very tight schedule. They need you to do well so that they have a good cast for their show. Therefore, be prepared to respond and perform on time and on cue, and think positively about this opportunity to demonstrate what you can do. If you don't get this part, remember that it is entirely possible that the reason you didn't get it may not necessarily be a reflection on your performance, but on what the panel were looking for and on who else they have already cast. If you have done a good audition you may be considered for other parts, or members of the panel may remember you when they see you again at other events in the future. Therefore, never go to an audition under-prepared, so that you can always perform at your best, even though you may not be right for the part.

CHOOSING YOUR MATERIAL

You need to have a portfolio of songs and speeches prepared for auditions. Within the portfolio you should have a variety of material that shows off your talents but that is suitable for a variety of situations. Try to avoid singing a song from the show you are auditioning for unless specifically asked to prepare it. The director, musical director and producer will have an idea of how they want that character to sound and behave, and in a first audition when you are unlikely to receive direction you could respond to, it is a bad idea to pre-empt this. If asked to return for a second or subsequent audition, you are more likely to be asked to prepare something from the show, which you should do as thoroughly as possible, and from memory if possible (though keep the score in front of you), so that you know the song well enough to respond to direction on the spot.

Preparing for an Audition

Do not learn new material for each audition – you will never be well-enough prepared for the nerves of the situation and will never show yourself off to advantage. The only time you should learn new material for an audition is when the director, producer or musical director asks you to learn something and invites you to come back for a recall to sing the music they have suggested – usually from the show they are casting. Then everybody understands that the material is new to you and that you may not be entirely confident with the words (though you should endeavour to be as confident as possible).

That means that you should assess the sorts of parts for which you are realistically likely to be considered and prepare yourself with suitable material for those types of projects. For example, if you are an attractive young man or woman and likely to be cast as juveniles or hero/ines, prepare that repertoire, but if you have a particularly strong pop sound, make sure you include something that demonstrates that side of your talent. If you are more likely to be cast in character or comedy roles, make sure that you have material that demonstrates both your vocal range and ability and your area of expertise. At the same time, remember that some auditions are for whole seasons, which might include a musical, a pantomime and other concerts or plays. You need some material that is a little more all-encompassing for these situations – this is where the up-tempo or point song and ballad combination is most useful. Throughout this book I've introduced you to a range of material for different situations. Now is the time to take a long hard look at yourself and your prospects and put together a suitable portfolio of at least eight different types of songs from a range of eras and genres, but always material sung by characters of your age, sex and type.

Many young singers pick songs that are emotionally complex and draining for their audition portfolio. While these are extremely good songs to learn in order to develop your technique, they are not necessarily good audition songs. As long as it is appropriate in style for the part, it is always good to sing something that gives you joy and that people can sit back and enjoy. You will look good singing it and the panel will remember your audition with pleasure. The really heavy or emotional songs are

Kristin Blaikie singing from the heart with no props, and an open face and body.

very difficult to perform on a cold November morning at 9am in a dark and dusty rehearsal space. It is almost impossible to create the right atmosphere in these circumstances, especially as you will have to walk into a difficult situation and get straight into the right emotional state. Moreover, the panel will be listening to an awful lot of songs during the course of the day; give them something to appreciate and enjoy.

In general, avoid mime and the use of major props, though small props such as a book, a newspaper or a chair (if one is in the space) could be used. Try to pick a song that doesn't rely on props but demonstrates your communication skills within the chosen style. In your preparation for the audition, ask a friend to watch your performance and comment on any particular hand gestures or physical movements you overuse, you need to be aware of these because with the nerves of an audition they will become exaggerated. Find a position that looks relaxed but doesn't block your body – so don't fold your arms or cross them in front of you except for a special desired effect. The old-fashioned position with your hands clasped in front of you at about waist height is a safe neutral position, if standing with your arms beside you makes you feel too vulnerable. However, once you get into the performance and become focused, your technique and your body will simply work in support of the emotions and ideas you are trying to communicate.

Once you have chosen and prepared your portfolio, use the songs in it for all your auditions, though you should continue to learn new songs that may become part of your portfolio when they are sufficiently rehearsed and have been repeatedly performed. The point is that if you have a good portfolio it will fit you for most first auditions and knowing your material really well will make the audition less nerve-racking.

PREPARING YOURSELF

Unless told differently by your agent or in the advert for the auditions, dress in smart casuals appropriate to the character. That doesn't mean that if you are auditioning for the plant in *Little Shop of Horrors* you should dress as a plant, but that you should look smart and prepared but in keeping with the style of the show. So, for example, you might dress more formally for an operetta audition and less formally for a repertory theatre season. However, first impressions do count, and you want to present the image of someone who is professional and reliable, as well as a good performer, so don't make the mistake of thinking that

your usual comfortable rehearsal clothes will suffice, unless you are asked to bring rehearsal clothes for a dance audition. Even then, make sure that they are smart. At the same time, you need to be comfortable, especially in your shoes, so find an audition outfit that works for you, but that also signifies that you are professional and reliable.

Since it is likely that the first thing you will be asked to do, after what may be a long journey and a considerable delay, is to sing, you must make sure that you find ways of warming up your voice and body. Work out the plan for your day that includes knowing when and where you are going to eat, carrying fruit and water with you so that you are prepared for delays, and knowing when and where you will be able to warm-up. You may decide to do a thorough warm-up at home and then just do a shorter, focusing session in an adjoining space

Cast of **Robinson Crusoe** *at the Yvonne Arnaud Theatre, Guildford (1990) at the end of their pre-performance warm-up.*

or even in the toilets of the venue. If this is not possible (and some venues are too echoey for this to be a realistic possibility), it may be a good idea to rent a music studio close to the audition venue for half-an-hour shortly before your audition time. Don't forget to warm-up and release the tensions in your body, as they will be exaggerated by the audition nerves.

Finally, in the excitement of arrival at the venue, meeting other auditionees, some of whom you may know from other shows or from training, don't forget the reason you are there. It is very easy to get caught up in chatting to other people and lose the focus and concentration you arrived with. Give yourself some time to focus your mind, to think through your material but also to prepare your mind to give the impression of yourself that you want to convey. Every audition is your most important performance, because it is not only a performance of your material, but of your professional attitude and mental approach.

AT THE AUDITION

When you are called into the audition you may be introduced and told either to sit down for a conversation or asked to sing first. If you are not introduced, introduce yourself clearly. This is the first opportunity the panel has to look at you and to hear you. Speak confidently and go forward to shake hands if the panel is on the same level as you. If you are on a stage, announce yourself and the song or songs you have brought. It may be appropriate to ask which song the panel wants to hear first, and asking may break the ice, but don't engage in long conversations or suggest every song in your portfolio. Merely ask what they want to hear, then introduce it, speak to the pianist

and when everyone is ready signal to the pianist that you are ready to begin.

Most importantly, do not apologize for the state of your music, your voice, your dress or anything else. Everyone who walks into the room has reasons why they are not going to give the best performance they are capable of, but it is your job to be prepared to do just that in any circumstances whatever – that is what performing in a musical show requires. In most cases, any loss of vocal ability is psychosomatic or the result of poor preparation and nerves. If you have genuinely lost your voice through illness, phone ahead and ask to postpone the audition. If that is not possible and you decide to go ahead with the audition, you may explain the situation but remember that the panel hears the same excuses from everyone, so be judicious with explanations unless there is a genuinely serious problem.

When asked to sing, which may or may not be at the start of the audition, give the music to the accompanist, explain any markings you have made on the score and give them a sense of the tempo you will be singing the music at; some songs, like, for example, 'Fish gotta swim', can be sung as a slow blues or quite fast. Again, I stress that the pianist will do their best to help you, but you must make that possible by having clearly marked and legible music in the correct key. Find a good place to stand where you can be clearly seen and heard. Do not stand behind the pianist or attempt to read the words either from the music score or from a crib sheet. You must be able to perform fully, and this is only possible from memory. Check that you are in light or, if lit by daylight, that you are not standing with the sun behind you so that you are only seen in silhouette. When you, and the panel, are ready, nod to the pianist who will begin the

Preparing Your Music

You need the music that you are going to sing, to be in a printed format so that it is easily legible to the accompanist who may be reading this piece of music for the first time. In fact, most regular audition pianists know the repertoire extremely well, but you need to make it as easy as possible for them to give you the best accompaniment, which will increase your confidence and improve your performance.

If you are doing the repeats as written in the score, only doing certain verses or want to make cuts or pauses in your performance, mark the score accordingly so that the accompanist can follow you. Make sure that the pianist does not have to keep turning multiple pages back and forth and that the book you present will stay open on the music stand. This may involve photocopying some, or all, of the piece so that you can mount it on card or put it into a ring binder in cellophane pockets back to back, so that both sides of the page can be read. Unmounted or unbound photocopies tend to slide off the stand. If the piece is unusually long and can't be mounted flat, make it into a book in which there are no repeats beyond the previous page.

introduction. Stand comfortably during the introduction, creating the atmosphere for the start of the song; this is something you must prepare. Equally, at the end of the song, maintain the mood of your performance until the final note of the playout has fallen silent. Then thank the pianist who has shared that moment of performance with you.

When you are singing, you need to find an appropriate focus and stance, movement and gesture for the song. Obviously these will vary according to the song; a ballad is likely to be addressed over the heads of the panel and require an internal focus from the singer, while a comedy song might occasionally be addressed in the direction of the panel, but do not attempt to catch the eyes of panel members and sing directly to them. The panel members want to feel comfortable looking at you and assessing your powers of communication to a wider audience, as well as your technical ability. They can't do this if you make them feel uneasy by looking directly at them. However, your eyes need to remain alive, so, even if you maintain a fixed point of focus, you need to imagine what you are seeing in your mind's eye and allow that to be communicated in your face.

My final words of advice to you are to enjoy the opportunity of singing the song you have chosen, which demonstrates your vocal ability and your joy in performing.

AFTER THE AUDITION

Thank the audition panel and the pianist before leaving the audition. If you have not already been told, ask about the time-scale in which the panel will be making decisions, so that you know whether you (or your agent) are expecting a phone call that day or in three weeks. Whatever you think of your own performance, do not apologize. After the audition, take some time to reflect. What might you improve on? How might you appear more relaxed and confident? What was the effect of nerves on your voice and how could you improve your preparation to counter that? This is not the opportunity to beat yourself up, but to assess your performance and develop your ability to audition well.

You should also make some notes about

Teddie Thomson and Janie Dee in the dressing room getting ready, mentally and physically, for their performances in A Chorus of Disapproval *at Salisbury Playhouse (1987).*

what you performed, who you met and how it went. You can do this immediately or later in the day when you have had a chance to calm down and think coherently, but it is a useful record that you can refer to when thinking about what to sing for your next audition, and when deciding what to sing next time you meet one of those panel members.

If you are invited for a recall, congratulate yourself on your success, but then treat it with just as much seriousness and professionalism as the first audition. Prepare yourself thoroughly, make sure you are warmed up and relaxed because each stage is harder than the last. But remember, if you have got through the early rounds it means that your ability is not in doubt, the decision is now about the balance of casting in the production, as much as the indi-viduals. So enjoy each opportunity to perform and to progress, and learn from every encounter.

TAKING CARE OF YOUR VOICE

During the normal course of events, everyday speaking or occasional singing, your voice will not come under any undue stress if you use it without unnecessary tension. It is designed for activity and using the muscles improves their flexibility. However, the much greater activity and stress of using the voice for high-volume singing or for many hours of rehearsal can cause tiredness. When the vocal cords become swollen through tiredness or irritation they actually contain more water. This causes them

131

to be more inflexible, but also more tender and susceptible to permanent tissue damage.

The vocal cords will recover from tiredness with rest, sleep and hydration, but this is sometimes difficult to achieve if there is an imminent performance. Rest means healthy sleep but it also means vocal rest, that is stopping speaking and singing completely, even for only a short while. So, if you are becoming vocally tired, it is important to protect your voice by stopping speaking completely, whenever possible, outside the rehearsal room. Speaking over other noises, especially in cars, pubs or clubs is particularly harmful, as the attempt to speak louder can lead to pushing the voice, so be careful in busy and crowded places or where there is the noise of machines.

During the rehearsal, if your voice is becoming very tired, with the agreement of the director and musical director, you could 'mark' the vocal delivery, leaving more vocal energy for the performance. 'Marking' requires that you act physically at the level of the performance, and vocally that you perform with a clear tone and range of dynamics, correct pace and feel, but that the volume of the voice is maintained at about half its usual level. In many ways, 'marking' is difficult to achieve effectively, because it is very easy to get carried away and to perform at full level, or to give insufficient performance level for other performers to work effectively with you. However, it can be necessary before a heavy performance or during a run of performances.

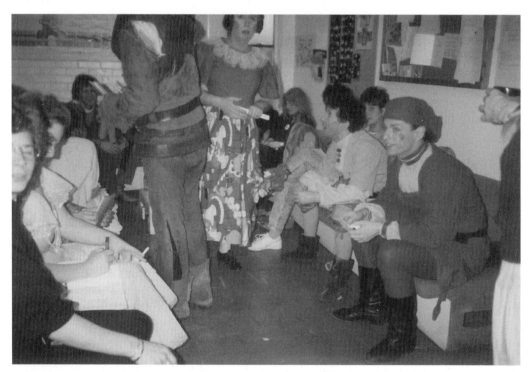

In the green room at Salisbury Playhouse, receiving notes after the dress rehearsal of Jack and the Beanstalk *(1987).*

If the vocal work you are doing requires shouting or screaming, you must take the same care as you would for belting or for other high-stress activities. Make sure you have warmed-up sufficiently, drink plenty of fluids when practising, don't rehearse for long periods at a time and use some simple humming and sirening exercises to cool the voice down afterwards.

Hydration is important to the physical well-being of the body, but it is particularly important for the singer. Mucus is formed in the respiratory system to clean and lubricate it. The mucus can become thick and sticky, especially, for example, when you have a cold. This mucus is normally so thin that it doesn't affect you, but when you become aware of it, as during a cold, it can be thinned by drinking plenty of fluid. The most effective liquids for hydration of the voice are water and warm drinks that contain no alcohol or caffeine. Both alcohol and caffeine dry the vocal folds and contribute to the problem of irritation.

The worst thing you can do at any time is to smoke or go to smoky places and inhale other people's cigarette fumes. The heat and irritation from smoking can cause dryness and irritation of the respiratory tract and vocal folds, which will affect the vocal quality by causing stiffness in the folds, and will reduce your ability to breathe in long controlled phrases. The chemical effects from the ingredients in the cigarettes contribute to the stiffening of the folds and can cause permanent damage. Of course, that is apart from the potential smoking has for increasing the risk of cancer and heart disease. It is now well-documented that passive smoking also has similar

The cast of The Rocky Horror Show *before a publicity appearance in Budapest.*

effects on the lungs and respiratory tract, so avoid smoking and smokers, whenever possible.

Equally, you should be aware of other dusty and polluted environments. Avoid them if possible but, if you can't, try to mitigate their effects by breathing through the nose, as the nose acts as a filter. This is not possible when singing, though, so be aware of the environment you are in. If dryness and dust can't be avoided (as in most theatres), then continue to re-hydrate as much as possible. Central heating and air conditioning are both drying to the voice, so you need to keep sipping water to maintain a healthy level of hydration when working in those environments, and in cold weather breathe through the nose as much as possible, as the nose acts as a radiator warming the air before it reaches the throat. The most important thing overall, however, is to maintain your physical well-being through healthy diet, exercise and plenty of sleep. If you are healthy, you will be more likely to fight any infections and recover quickly from tiredness and stress.

So, after the excitement of the opening night go and enjoy yourself at the party, but not too much if there is another performance to follow. Limit your alcohol intake in favour of water, avoid the smokers, don't say too much or sing along to the music and go home reasonably early to rest before your next performance. I promise you can still enjoy yourself, and you will enjoy your second performance all the more.

13 EPILOGUE

This book is intended to empower you to sing in the ways and in the environments you choose, whether professional, amateur, public or private, to open your throat, take a deep breath and make a big and joyous sound. I hope you now feel confident to do so. But it's hard to keep working on something alone, whether your intention is to perform professionally or whether you are singing for your own pleasure. So take every opportunity that presents itself to sing, especially with other people or for other people. Join a local choir so that you are constantly singing and practising, and so that your practice has a

Top hat routine from **Starting Here, Starting Now** *(Exeter, 1997).*

purpose and a focus. If there isn't a local choir, what about a close harmony group? It is really useful to learn to sing harmonies. And if none of those is available, why not get together with some friends and start your own group, singing the music you enjoy? You could sing songs from the shows as well as popular classics or whatever you like, and I guarantee you will be in demand to perform at local community events. Find an accompanist or see if you can find a backing track on the internet, and go and sing in hospitals or in care homes, you will be enormously appreciated.

Or take it a step further still and, once you have got your singing group off the ground, organize your own community event with local performers of all types, and join the local amateur dramatic society and experience the thrill of creating a character for yourself. The important thing is to keep your voice working, and keep sharing it with others. Sing around the house, but also sing for others at every opportunity. Sing at weddings, at funerals, at local festivals and family celebrations. Make singing an expression of your enjoyment of life.

I spoke at the start of this book about the benefits of breathing, releasing the tensions in the body, making sounds and communicating. I hope that you have felt those benefits while working through this book, and that you now take the opportunity to include singing as an important social and performative activity in your life.

Wishing you good luck, good vocal health, and great enjoyment.

A Few Words of Thanks

The idea for this book came from a conversation with Tony Britten and Mary Lincoln. While writing this book I've had a lot of help from the Research and Knowledge Transfer Committee at the University of Winchester, who funded some of the time to write this, and from my colleagues who discussed ideas and supported my endeavours. Friends and family are always supportive, especially in allowing me to disappear socially for periods of time while writing. Most important in the development of this book, however, are the numerous directors, choreographers, actors and singers who I worked with during twenty years as a professional vocal coach, musical director and director. They have stimulated the development of my ideas. Some of those people are included in the photos in this book, taken in a rather haphazard fashion during my professional career, never imagining that they would see the light of day. Special thanks go to two of my current students, Emma Shearmur and Jennifer Lloyd, who gave up a sunny morning to pose for photographs for this book, and to the group of music theatre students who responded enthusiastically to trying out these exercises to make sure they understood them from the words I'd written.

FURTHER INFORMATION

SUGGESTIONS FOR FURTHER READING

Berry, C. (1980 [1973]) *Voice and the Actor.* Harrap: London.

Bunch D. M. (2005) *The Performer's Voice: Realizing your Vocal Potential.* W.W.Norton: New York and London.

Bunch, M. (1997) *The Dynamics of the Singing Voice.* Springer: Wien and New York.

Cook, O. (2004) *Singing With Your Own Voice.* Nick Hern Books: London.

de Mallet Burgess, T. and Skilbeck, N. (2000) Routledge: London.

Kayes, G. (2000) *Singing and the Actor.* A&C Black: London.

Linklater, K. (1976) *Freeing the Natural Voice.* Drama Book Publishers: New York.

Melton, J. Tom, K (2003) *One Voice: Integrating Singing Technique and Theatre Voice Training.* Heinemann: Portsmouth N.H.

Nelson, S. H. (2002) *Singing with Your Whole Self: The Feldenkrais Method and Voice.* Scarecrow: London.

VOCAL SCORES OR VOCAL SELECTIONS

Below are listed the vocal scores or vocal selections referred to in the book.

Cabaret, John Kander and Fred Ebb, score and vocal selections from the film.

Chicago, John Kander and Fred Ebb, score and vocal selections from the film.

City of Angels, Cy Coleman, David Zippel and Larry Gelbart, vocal score.

Dreamgirls, Henry Krieger and Tom Eyen, vocal selections.

Evita, Andrew Lloyd Webber and Tim Rice, musical excerpts.

Grease, Warren Casey and Jim Jacobs, vocal selections.

Guys and Dolls, Frank Loesser, vocal score.

Gypsy, Jule Styne, Stephen Sondheim and Arthur Laurents, vocal score.

Into the Woods, Stephen Sondheim and James Lapine, vocal score.

Jesus Christ Superstar, Andrew Lloyd Webber and Tim Rice.

Kiss me Kate, Cole Porter and Sam and Bella Spewack, vocal score.

Little Shop of Horrors, Alan Menken and Howard Ashman, vocal selections from the film.

Mack and Mabel, Jerry Herman and Michael Stewart, vocal selections.

Man of La Mancha, Mitch Leigh and Joe Darion, vocal score.

Mikado, The, W. S. Gilbert and Arthur Sullivan, vocal score.

My Fair Lady, Alan Jay Lerner and Frederick Loewe, vocal score.

Oklahoma!, Richard Rodgers and Oscar Hammerstein, vocal score.

Pirates of Penzance, The, W. S. Gilbert and Arthur Sullivan, vocal score.

Rocky Horror Show, Richard O'Brien, vocal selections.

Show Boat, Jerome Kern and Oscar Hammerstein, vocal score.

Starting Here, Starting Now, Richard Maltby Jr and David Shire, vocal selections.

Sweeney Todd, Stephen Sondheim and Hugh Wheeler, vocal score.

West Side Story, Leonard Bernstein, Stephen Sondheim and Arthur Laurents, vocal score.

SONG COLLECTIONS

All Sondheim (four volumes). Warner Bros Publications.

The Best of George Gershwin. Chappell and Co.: London (1976).

Music and Lyrics by Cole Porter. Chappell and Co.: New York.

The Stephen Sondheim Songbook. Chappell and Co.: London (1979).

Too Many Songs by Tom Lehrer. Methuen (1981).

SOURCES OF MUSIC, BOOKS, CDS AND DVDS

Dress Circle is the main supplier for CDs and DVDs of musicals. They also have a stock of books and scores. The shop is at:

57–59 Monmouth Street London WC2H 9DG.

Tel: 0207 224 2227.

www.dresscircle.co.uk.

Chappell of Bond Street (which has moved to 152–160 Wardour Street in London's Soho) is the main supplier of music scores and sheet music. The online shop is at: www.chappellofbondstreet.co.uk.

Tel: 0207 100 6126 (Select Option 1).

For books about musical theatre go to the Royal National Theatre bookshop in London (in the National Theatre on London's South Bank – 5 minutes walk from Waterloo Station) or look online at www.Amazon.co.uk.

INDEX OF MUSICAL EXAMPLES

INDEX OF ILLUSTRATIONS

INDEX

INDEX